Raising Sunshine

A Guide to Parenting Through the Aftermath of Infant Death

Ariane E. Sroubek, Psy.D.

For my Sunshine daughter and Rainbow son
and for their sibling prayer warriors who have gone home before them.
And for my husband, my safe port on this journey to Heaven.

"Love and sacrifice are closely linked, like the sun and the light. We cannot love without suffering. We cannot suffer without love."

-St. Gianna Beretta Molla

Contents

PREFACE

"Perfect relief is not possible, except with time. You cannot now realize that you will ever feel better. Is not this so? And yet it is a mistake. You are sure to be happy again. To know this, which is certainly true, will make you some less miserable now. I have had experience enough to know what I say..."
- Abraham Lincoln

On a steamy afternoon in Hodgenville, Kentucky, a young boy sat on a bench in front of a rough log cabin, rhythmically swinging his bare feet. He was tall but his clothes indicated that he was only three or four years old. He turned his head toward his father's work shed and listened to the drum of a hammer striking wood. Then he turned back toward the cabin door where he heard bits of conversation drifting out past him and into the vegetable patch that stretched out in front of his home.

The cabin was busy. Too busy. Women he knew from church began coming at dawn, bringing food, advice, tears, and comfort for the boy's distraught mother. The first one to arrive found the boy curled in a corner near his mother's bed. The woman had picked him up gently, spoke softly and then sent the boy outside to play, but the boy did not feel like playing.

He frowned and his dark eyebrows almost touched as he tried to make sense of what was happening. His baby brother was dead, and that reality paralyzed him. A tear pushed its way out of the corner of the boy's eye and wound its way slowly down his hot cheek as he thought about the things he would never do with the infant that lay, unmoving inside the cabin.

Suddenly, the boy's thoughts were interrupted by the sight of his playmate running down the path towards him. His grief was instantly forgotten as he stood up and, smiling, ran off to play with the boy. There would be time to grieve and remember his brother later but, at that moment, the magic of childhood was too strong for him to resist.

Nearly fifty years later, the boy, grown into man, sat at a high desk as he recorded the story of his life. He paused and gazed into the shadows of a room that was barely illuminated by the small candle beside him. His face was thoughtful, and his dark eyebrows furrowed as they had done so many years ago on the bench outside of his family's cabin. The man's expression reflected tremendous effort, as if he was trying to condense an ocean of memories onto a single page. Finally, he nodded slightly and, dipping his pen into the inkwell, returned to his work.

On the page before him, he wrote "I had a brother, younger than myself, who died in infancy." The man nodded again as if he was satisfied with what he had written and then continued to write the story of how he had grown from the boy on the bench into America's 16th president. In his own quiet and unassuming way, the man ensured that history would know that his baby brother, who died just days after his birth, had been an unforgettable part of his life – the life of Abraham Lincoln.[1]

—   —   —   —   —   —   —   —   —   —   —

Parents[2] who lose a baby are immediately faced with the question "How do we tell our living children that their sibling has died?" Soon, more questions follow. They wonder and worry "How do we help our children through their grief?" "How do we guide them through the funeral and other death rituals?" and "How do we parent while we are consumed by our own grief?" Central to these questions is a parent's deep love for their sunshine (living) child coupled with the fear that this child will be irreparably damaged by sibling loss.

What is a Sunshine Child?
In the infant loss community, a child who is born before a loss is often called a sunshine child because they were born before the storm of child death when the world seemed sunny. Children born after a loss are called rainbow babies because they are like the

rainbow after a storm. In this book, I use the term sunshine child/children whenever I refer to siblings who were born before a loss.

Unfortunately, bereaved parents often find few resources to help them navigate this challenging time. I wrote this book to provide practical suggestions and insight into childhood grief so that parents can walk alongside their beloved children as they journey together through loss. I hope that, in addition to practical advice and information, this book will provide parents with hope, encouragement and the certainty that they are not alone. In developed countries, five to eight percent of children with siblings experience the death of a brother or sister during their childhood. Since one in four pregnancies end in loss, the number of children losing a sibling is even higher when miscarriages are included in the number of lost siblings. While the death of a sibling is traumatic and certainly plays a role in their development, many children overcome and even thrive in the face of such loss. In fact, some of history's most well-known figures lost a sibling during their childhood, including Abraham Lincoln, Sigmund Freud, St. John Paul II, Eleanor Roosevelt, Mark Twain, Charles Dickens, and St. Kateri Tekakwitha. These giants of history were able to overcome their grief and to become figures who are recognized for their unique strength, insight, creativity, passion, and compassion. In fact, many of them, like Freud, found that their loss led them to their greatest ideas.

While all of this is true, it is also true that sibling loss has a profound effect on child development. As one group of researchers[3] wrote, "(sibling loss) is clearly an experience that appears to have lifelong implications." For parents and caregivers who are grieving themselves, helping a grieving child to navigate sibling loss can be an overwhelming task. Unfortunately, rather than providing parents with encouragement, most of the research that has been done on sibling loss emphasizes the vulnerability of sunshine children rather than focusing on their capacity for growth, resilience, and strength. Grieving families do not need another litany of the potential risks that sunshine children face. Instead, they need hope that their sunshine children can weather the storm of sibling loss. I wrote this book to meet this need.

The tools, suggestions and research recorded on these pages are meant to support you, the caregiver, as you navigate this new and likely unexpected phase of your parenting journey. They are meant to encourage you, reassure you of your sunshine child's resiliency, and provide you with evidence-based information and suggestions about navigating your child's grief journey. Most importantly, this book was written to remind you that you are not alone. Each year, the parents of nearly two million children join you on this journey of parenting after the death of an infant. The path through grief is one that we all walk together as we learn how to raise our sunshine children. My hope is that this book can help and comfort you as you travel through your family's profound loss.

SECTION I: THE FIRST DAYS

"I will not say: do not weep; for not all tears are evil."
-J.R.R. Tolkien, *The Return of the King*

I will never forget the moment when I looked up at the doctor from the operating table and heard him say the words "I'm so sorry." My mind could not comprehend what he was saying and, yet my heart somehow did understand as it splintered into millions of pieces. Those words shattered my world and forever divided my life into the time before loss and the time after loss. Words like "devastated," "crushed," and "heartbroken" do not even come close to describing the emotions of that moment. Only Zoe Clark-Coates's description begins to convey what it was like: "The doctor said you had gone. In that moment, my world went silent."

In the midst of my agony, I knew that I was still the mother of a little sunshine child who was anxiously waiting for news that her sister had been born. I struggled to quickly fit together pieces of my broken self so that I could continue mothering her. I worried about how we could tell her that her sister, Noemi, would never be coming home. I wondered what she would understand. Mostly, though, I struggled to figure out how I could help her to survive this storm that had left so much destruction in my own heart. How could I keep the horror that threatened to destroy me from damaging her?

In the weeks between Noemi's death and her funeral, I drew on every bit of my knowledge of child psychology as I struggled to help my preschooler through her sister's death. I needed to take concrete steps to get through those early days. I needed to know how to talk to my sunshine daughter about her experience of loss, its meaning in light of our faith, and the significance of various rituals of death. I needed to understand how to help her navigate grief and make sense of what was happening. Most importantly, I needed to learn how our family could begin living again while we mourned the tiny life that had ended.

It is my goal that the first section of this book will provide you with the knowledge that I craved during those first weeks after Noemi's death. I hope that it will prepare you for the difficult conversations that lie ahead, help you make decisions about how much to involve your sunshine child in rituals of loss, and give you confidence as you guide your child through events that can seem confusing and overwhelming.

As a mother who has walked the road on which you now walk, my deepest hope for you is that, during all of the challenges that you will face over these first few days and weeks, you will be able to offer yourself grace. You will inevitably make mistakes and you may have regrets, but at the end of the day, what will matter is your love for your sunshine child and your willingness to be there for them no matter what life throws at you. I once heard a mother say that good parenting is about doing our best and trusting that God will fill in the gaps for us when we fall short. Whether you believe that there is a God or not, my hope is that as you read the following pages and begin to implement what you learn in your own life, you will be able to trust that your best is enough.

CHAPTER ONE: TALKING WITH YOUR SUNSHINE CHILD

"At heart, we prefer to deny that there is any connection between death and our children. Nonetheless, experience does not allow us to maintain this denial for very long."
– Helen Rosen

When Noemi died, we immediately asked ourselves how we would tell our Sunshine that her hoped for sister would never come home. Telling her the truth went against our instinct to protect her, but, in the context of sibling loss, we had no choice. While we would have liked to spare our sunshine child from the knowledge that her sister had died, doing so was impossible.

Still, many families are tempted to cover up or minimize sibling loss. In fact, a survey of adults found that, as recently as the 1980s, sixty-two percent of bereaved siblings did not discuss their sibling's death with their families. Yet, research tells us that one of the most important things parents can do is to talk with sunshine children about their sibling's loss. As difficult as it is, having this conversation is necessary.

Due to my medical situation, my mother was the one who told our sunshine that Noemi was dead. As a social worker, she knew how to share the information in a way that my daughter could understand and she let my Sunshine take the lead on how much information to share. I do not know much about what happened during that first conversation, but when I asked my Sunshine about it years later, she recalled two things: she was very sad and her grandparents let her snuggle between them until she fell asleep. In other words, she remembers her grief and she remembers being comforted. Her response reminded me that what we say and how we say it doesn't matter nearly as much as our willingness to be with our children through their grief.

As you or your family member prepare to talk to your sunshine child about your baby's death, it can be helpful to keep the following in mind:

1. Talk As Soon As Possible

Studies show that children do best when they are given time to prepare for a sibling's death. In fact, children who participate in caring for their sibling and engage in preparations for their death are better able to cope with their loss. Families with advanced warning that something is wrong with their baby may even choose to find a therapist or other professional who can begin working with their sunshine children so that they already have an established relationship when the baby dies.

Unfortunately, because infant deaths are often unexpected, such preparation is often impossible. However, it is still important to talk to your sunshine child as soon as possible. Children are curious and have active imaginations. When they do not have information, they tend to creatively fill in gaps in their knowledge themselves and this can lead to confusion and distress. Additionally, when you are quick to talk with your child, they know that they can trust you to tell them what they need to know, when they need to know it. As a result, they are less likely to worry that you might be withholding information from them in the future.

2. Be Focused

Get right to the point and then let your child guide the rest of the conversation with their own questions. Stay focused on what your child needs to know and what their questions tell you they want to know. It is important for your sunshine child to understand that their sibling died, so address that fact right at the beginning of your conversation. However, they do not necessarily need to know the details surrounding their sibling's death. Once you have said that the baby died, wait for them to ask questions and do not offer information that they do not ask about. By letting your sunshine child guide the conversation with their questions, you give them the space to get more information if they need it, while also shielding them from unhelpful details that might upset them.

3. Use Clear and Simple Language

Children are often confused by the words that adults use to discuss death. As adults, we do not like to use direct language when talking about death. Instead, we try to soften the impact of what we are saying by using euphemisms like "we lost the baby," "the baby was born sleeping," and "the baby passed away." However, children need clear and straightforward language to help them understand what is happening and to avoid misunderstanding, since they interpret language literally.

For example, a child might hear you say that the baby was "lost" and think that his or her sibling can be found again or that the baby was carelessly left somewhere. It would be better if you said "I have some sad news to share with you. Our baby was too sick to live and he died. We are unhappy, but mommy and daddy are ok. We love you very much and are here to help you," While such an introduction might sound too abrupt in an adult conversation, it would be helpful to a sunshine child.

4. Be Honest

During these first conversations about your baby's death, being honest can help you and your sunshine child to communicate openly in the future. It will also help them to trust you as they navigate their grief. Developing this trusting relationship with your sunshine child is particularly important because sibling death makes a child's world feel unpredictable and unsafe. It is critical that they know that you are a safe person who they can depend on, even as you are dealing with your own sorrow.

In our family, I promised my Sunshine that I would never lie to her. This promise was challenged a few weeks after our loss when my daughter began asking questions. "Is Heaven real?" she asked, and I answered that it was. Then she followed up with, "Is God real?" I nodded. "Is Santa Claus real?" Until that moment, I had no intention of telling my three-year-old that Santa was not real. I had envisioned years of magical Christmases before I would need to address that question. However, I also knew that I had promised not to lie to my daughter and, particularly given the context of the question, I knew that she needed me to be honest. So, I told her the truth. Remarkably, she still enjoyed many magical Christmases because, apparently, imagining that Santa is real is just as good as believing that he is. More importantly, however, she trusted me about the things that really mattered and now, half a decade later, she still trusts in my promise to always be truthful. Just this morning, she told my son, "Mommy never lies." I am grateful that she trusts me. It is a wonderful foundation for our relationship.

5. Don't Hesitate to Say That You Don't Know

Your child might ask questions that, for any number of reasons, are impossible to answer. For example, our daughter wanted to know what caused Noemi's death, but since this was initially unclear, we had to wait to get that information from her autopsy. In situations like these, part of being honest is being willing to tell your child that you do not know the answer to their questions. Just like a patient trusts a doctor who says, "I am not sure what is going on so I am going to refer you to someone who does," children trust parents who say, "I don't know but I will do my best to find out."

If your child asks a question that you will never be able to answer, you might want to say something like:

"I don't know, but I wonder if ...."
"I don't know, let's think about that together."
"I don't know the answer to that, let's ask our priest/pastor/other trusted advisor."
"I don't know. What do you think?"

Some questions do not have answers that we can ever be sure of and it is not unusual for children to ask these types of questions after a baby dies. Curiosity about pain, death, the afterlife, and God is common in bereaved children and adults. It is not unusual for even very young children to ask questions about these things. It is best to let your child know that there are some questions that cannot be answered. This teaches them to be comfortable with the unanswered questions that are an inescapable part of life.

6. Check for Understanding

Sometimes, a child's understanding of a conversation is very different from what was actually said. It is important for parents to ensure that their sunshine child understands what is being discussed. How your sunshine child responds can offer clues about what they understand. For example, if a child says "The baby died because it was sick. My friend Johnny is sick. Does that mean he is going to die too?" then the parents have an opportunity to help their child understand that there are different degrees of sickness, most of which do not result in death.

In addition to carefully listening to what a sunshine child says, parents should pay attention to their child's body language. Parents are often intuitively skilled at reading their child's non-verbal signals, so they may be able to tell how their child is processing the discussion just by watching him or her. If a child's body language does not match the content of your conversation, this could indicate a problem with their understanding. For example, an excited young child who is told that their baby died but continues to bounce up and down happily likely has not understood what they were told. Other body language might help parents to recognize that their sunshine child needs a break from talking or that they are feeling afraid, angry, or in need of a hug.

7. Try to Understand Their Emotions

Sunshine children have big emotions. Sometimes these feelings are confusing or even frightening. One of the most important reasons to talk with your child about their grief is to help you accurately assess and understand their feelings. This allows you to comfort, bond with, and more fully understand your child. As a result, you are better equipped to help them as they navigate their loss.

Unfortunately, children (and many adults) often have difficulty expressing their emotions. Young children may only identify basic emotions such as "happy," "sad," and "mad." They may also lack the vocabulary to express what they are feeling. In these situations, you can encourage your child to draw a picture or to use playdough to show you how they feel. Older children probably have the language to describe how they are feeling but may be confused by their emotions.

Some older children, like my Sunshine, are uncomfortable talking about their feelings. To help my daughter to feel more comfortable sharing her emotions, we play a variation of "Two Truths and a Lie." Each of us takes a turn saying two feelings that we are experiencing and one emotion that we do not currently feel. The other person guesses which feeling is the fake feeling. It is amazing how quickly this game can move a child from responding with "I don't know" to being engaged in a conversation about their emotions. It is also surprising how often we make incorrect assumptions about each other's emotions. This is a good reminder to listen to what our words and body language are conveying.

8. Let Your Child Guide the Conversation

Children are geniuses at letting us know how much they can and want to handle. As a result, one of the best ways to talk with Sunshines about the death of a sibling is to let them lead the conversation. This means asking open-ended questions and stopping when they are done.

Asking your sunshine child questions that require more than a "yes" or "no" reply helps to establish good communication and gives them the opportunity to steer the conversation so that it addresses the issues that are most important to them. It also helps you to understand them and their unique needs and perspectives. As a result, such questions help children to feel supported and heard by their parents. If you are not sure of what to ask, try one of these:

- ✓ "What are you thinking or feeling about this?"
- ✓ "What questions do you have about what I have been telling you?"
- ✓ "Can you tell me in your own words what we have been talking about?"

✓ "What are you most sad or angry about?"

✓ "What are you nervous about?"

✓ "Why does that feel scary to you?"

✓ "How can I help you right now?"

It can be scary and painful for parents to talk with their children about difficult topics, but when children ask about them it is often an indication that they are wrestling with these issues and we do not want our children to be struggling alone. Of course, if your child asks you a question that you are uncomfortable answering because of their age, it is alright to say, "I see that you are curious about that. Let's talk about it when you are older" or "I promise I will tell you someday, but you need to be older before we talk about that."

That being said, my experience has been that parents tend to underestimate what children are capable of understanding and it is important to know that withholding information comes at a cost. Children, especially those with active imaginations, tend to generate their own answers when we don't provide them with one. Often, the imagined answers are ultimately more disturbing to them than the truth would have been. As a result, I encourage you to let your child lead the conversation by answering even their hardest questions in age-appropriate ways.

We realized how critically important this was when our Sunshine asked why she could not see the color photos that were taken of her sister. We told her that she could see them when she was older, but she needed to wait to see them. Several months later, our Sunshine said something about her sister having a scary, green face. Confused, I asked her what she meant. She told me that she could not see the color photos because the baby's face was "all scary and green." I realized that our daughter had concluded something that was much more upsetting than the reality, so I brought out our color photo-album. My three-year-old browsed through them and said, "Oh, she didn't look scary." Then she happily ran off to play.

This rapid switch from a serious conversation to carefree play is not uncommon in children, and it is important that parents recognize their child's need to "take a break" from their grief for a while. This can be challenging because many parents have an idea about what they want to share with their sunshine child when they begin a conversation. As a result, parents who are focused on their goals might miss signals that their sunshine child needs a break.

In the same way that children can determine what information they need, they are also very good at figuring out when they have enough information. They use a variety of verbal and nonverbal signals to let parents know when they have reached this point and it is important for parents to respect these. Some children, like mine, have the verbal skills to say that they do not want to talk anymore. She would ask a question and then, once she was satisfied with the answer, hold up her little hand and say, "No more words now." Others might become restless and appear eager to go off and play. Still others might become goofy, make inappropriate or off topic remarks, or become quieter and more detached. You know your child best so when he or she shows signs that they are done talking, pay attention.

9. Expect the Conversation to be Ongoing

Do not worry if your child cannot handle all of the information that you want to share with them in one dose. Your first conversation will not be your last. Instead, think of this first talk as a single chapter in a much longer, ongoing conversation about the death.

It is worth underscoring the fact that children can only absorb so much information at once. They need time to process what you tell them and to think of new questions. Their emotions evolve over time and these changes raise different issues for them that they will need help understanding. Thus, your first discussion with your sunshine child sets the tone for future conversations.

Knowing this should alleviate some of the anxiety that you might have about talking with your child. You do not have to cover everything and explain it all perfectly in a single shot. In fact, it would be impossible to do so! There will be many opportunities in the future to expand and clarify.

Tips for Comforting Your Child as You Talk	
USE WORDS	• Let your child know that you see and accept their feelings. • Remind your child that they are safe right now and that specific steps are being taken to keep them safe. • Tell your child that their sibling's death was not their fault. • Emphasize your love for your child because they may feel displaced as you work through your own grief
USE TOUCH	• Research shows that physical contact increases feelings of security and decreases distress. • Hug your child. • Hold hands.

	• Put your arm over your child's shoulder.
	• Sit next to your child or face your child and touch their hand
USE THE ENVIRONMENT	• Ensure that your child is physically comfortable.
	• Talk when your child is well rested, alert, and attentive.
	• Choose cozy chairs.
	• Find a quiet spot.
	• Let your child snuggle with a comfort object.
	• Wrap your child in a soft, warm blanket.
	• Offer your child their favorite snack or drink after you have finished talking

10. Let Yourself Be Comforted

While this first conversation will probably be one of the most difficult that you have ever had, you may come away comforted. Your sunshine child loves you and, just as you care about their pain, they are deeply impacted by yours. As a result, it is likely that they will try to comfort you, even as you are comforting them. One study found that such mutual comfort was a common theme in memories shared by bereaved Black mothers.[4] The researchers wrote, "Talking with living children was also a source of comfort. The children's responses to the news about the loss tended to be honest, clear, innocent, and hopeful. Their words of encouragement were comforting to the women and helped bring a new perspective to the loss." Just as you will use this conversation to remind your child that they are not alone, it might remind you that you have a precious little companion by your side. Do not let your desire to protect your child keep you from accepting their companionship; many families find a surprising source of strength in the comfort given and received within the family unit.

Raising Sunshine

CHAPTER TWO: READING TOGETHER

"Reading a book aloud to someone is an intimate act. It recalls the tenderness and warmth we felt as children when our parents read to us."
– Barrett Rollins

"That's what literature is. It's the people who went before us, tapping out messages from the past, from beyond the grave, trying to tell us about life and death! Listen to them!"
- Connie Willis

As parents, we know that reading is good for our children. When we read with them, we strengthen our relationship, boost their vocabulary, make them more likely to be strong readers, and improve the chances that they will do well in school. Reading books about loss to sunshine children offers additional benefits such as showing them that they are not alone in their experiences, giving them the words they need to talk about their loss, offering new ways to understand death, and helping parents and children to share their grief. Miraculously, it does all these things in a non-threatening and comforting way. This is why snuggling up to read a book about loss is an ideal way to communicate with your sunshine child about your baby's death.

Why Read?

1. Your Child Is Not Alone

Although infant loss is fairly common, many sunshine children may not know other bereaved siblings. Reading about others who have lost brothers or sisters can help sunshine children to feel less isolated.

As we read to our sunshine daughter, we recognized that she always pointed out characters who experienced grief. She connected with these characters in a personal way and often talked with us about how their stories were similar to her own experiences. It was clear that these connections were important to her.

2. Biographies Offer Hope

As my daughter and I read the biographies of people who had survived the loss of a sibling, we realized that their stories did not end with their sibling's death. Instead, these people did amazing things partly because of their struggles. My daughter and I began to internalize the possibility that she could not only survive her sister's death but also become a better person because of it. As her mother, I found that these stories helped me to focus on my daughter's resilience. The hope that these stories kindled was something that we could celebrate together because it was not just unrealistic optimism - it was based on the real lives of people who had overcome similar tragedies.

3. Books Build Understanding

Often a sunshine child's first experience of death is that of their sibling. Despite their young age, sunshine children are presented with the fact that death is final, universal, and real. They grapple with these facts in ways that most of us do not until much later in life. Books can help children to build their understanding. When chosen carefully, the stories can meet children at their developmental level. As a result, books can help Sunshine's to explore and make sense of issues surrounding death.[5]

4. Stories Provide Distance

The emotions of grief are intense and often overpowering. When a child is overwhelmed, it is difficult for them to use the parts of their brains that help them process their experiences. As a result, they can benefit from emotional distance in order to make sense of what has happened. Books can offer children a way to approach the subject of death while maintaining a safe distance. Thus, they can be useful tools in helping children to process their grief without becoming overwhelmed. For example, for centuries, storytellers have used animals to teach painful moral and life lessons because children do not identify with stories about animals in the same way that they connect with stories about humans. As a result, a child's emotional reaction to animal stories is not as intense and the stories feel less threatening: the child can play the safe role of observer. Stories, then, can offer children the emotional distance needed to engage their whole brains in wrestling with their grief.

Clearly, books are a great tool for the parents of sunshine children, but how do you find the books that are right for them? Books about death in general are relatively easy to find, but it can be challenging to find books that specifically address infant loss. Still, your local library is the best place to start your search. They often have a whole section of books that deal with death. A child or youth librarian should be able to help you to find books that are appropriate for your child. They can also locate books at other libraries that you can borrow through inter-library loans. Support groups, grief centers, counselors and online infant loss communities can also be good places to find recommendations that might be helpful to your sunshine child. For your convenience, I have also included a list of books that I have used or had recommended to me in Appendix IV.

You may find that there are books that do not focus on infant death but address issues that your child is dealing with as they grieve. As I noted before, my daughter and I discovered that the biography section of our library contained many books about people who had experienced the death of a sibling (often an infant sibling) as a child. Similarly, many great works of fiction deal with themes of loss and mortality in ways that can help your child to explore their own thoughts, feelings, and beliefs.[6]

While many children enjoy reading with their parents, not all children do. If your child or teenager is not a big reader, there are other things you can do with them that will help in similar ways. For example, art in all forms is a wonderful teacher when it comes to emotions and many masterpieces were inspired by death and grief. Whether a particular type of music, visual art, spoken word, or theater resonates with your child, their interest can be the catalyst that helps them to process their feelings while serving as a conversation starter for you. You might even discover that your child is able to create their own art that encourages the expression of their own emotional responses to death. As you and your child enjoy art together, you will discover new ways to express your shared grief and develop a deeper understanding of one another. [7]

If your child is not moved by art or literature, nature itself offers us insights into life, death, and rebirth. Death is an intrinsic part of life here on earth and it surrounds us, often in ways that are beautiful and deeply touching. Consider the changing weather and what is lost and gained as each season moves from one into the next. Help your child to identify and make sense of the death observed in the natural world. Watch flowers bloom, fade, and turn to seeds which will sow next year's blooms. Wonder with them as they explore predator and prey relationships and then witness animal displays of grief. By helping them to explore our temporal world, you can enhance the way that they understand their own grief.

CHAPTER THREE: MEETING THE DECEASED SIBLING

"The two hardest things to say in life are hello for the first time and goodbye for the last."

– Moira Rogers

One of the first decisions that parents face when a baby dies is whether to have their sunshine child meet or see their sibling after death. [8] Often this decision is made in a hurry and parents may not have the time to weigh their options. This was the case for us. Some families, however, have advanced warning that their infant will die and, while this knowledge is a horrible burden, it allows them to consider whether or not to have the siblings meet. If you are making this decision, the following information may help you to discern what is best for your sunshine child.

Historically, families were able to choose how involved their children were when a baby died because the death usually occurred at home. However, when society shifted from home births to medically monitored births, hospital restrictions began to dictate whether sunshine siblings (and even parents) were able to spend time with their sick, dying, or deceased infants. These restrictions were often based less on medical necessity and more on the belief that bonding with these infants would increase the family's suffering.[9] As a result, adults did not consider the possibility that grieving siblings might benefit from meeting their infant brothers and sisters, although such a meeting would provide them with a chance to say goodbye.

Thankfully, today we know that meeting a deceased sibling can be an important step in a child's grief journey. Still, as your sunshine child's parent, it is up to you to determine if such a meeting is best for your child.

Allowing your sunshine child to meet their infant sibling, even after death, can be helpful because seeing the deceased body shows children the physical alterations that occur in death. This visual opportunity can highlight some of the differences between life and death which ultimately furthers Sunshine's understanding. For this reason, Ann Chalmers, the chief executive of the Child

Bereavement Trust, recommends that parents of children ages two and older give their sunshine children the option to see their deceased sibling. She believes that this helps siblings to make sense of their loss and begin to grasp its finality.

While my own sunshine child did not meet her sister, I can see how this might have been helpful for her because of my own response to Noemi's body. When she was still soft, warm, and pink, I had difficulty comprehending that she was dead. However, as she grew colder and her color became more ashen, the reality of her death began to sink in. By the time I let go of Noemi for the last time, her physical condition had convinced me that some essential part of her was no longer present.

As the parent of your sunshine child, you are in the best position to determine whether such a meeting would be helpful or harmful for your child. There are certainly legitimate reasons that parents might choose not to facilitate such a meeting. As you weigh the costs and benefits for your family, it can be helpful to think about the following:

1. Yourself

It is wise to consider your own health – emotional and physical - and your responses to your baby's death. You may want to ask yourself:

- ✓ How do I tend to react to grief and stress?
- ✓ How am I currently reacting to the baby's death?
- ✓ Can I move beyond my own emotions to comfort my sunshine child?
- ✓ Am I medically stable enough to be available to my sunshine child?
- ✓ Is there another trusted adult who can take my place if I am unable to be there for my child right now?
- ✓ How will I feel witnessing my children meeting?
- ✓ If your infant has not yet died: Will I be able to share the short time I have with my baby?

2. Your Child

The age, personality, and unique development of your sunshine child is an important consideration in deciding whether to introduce the siblings. The following questions might help to clarify whether your child would benefit from meeting your infant:

- ✓ How does my child feel about meeting the baby? Do they want to participate in this introduction? [10]
- ✓ If the death was expected: How has my child been coping with the pending loss?
- ✓ If the death was sudden and without warning: Will I have time to prepare my child to see the baby?
- ✓ Is my sunshine child very young? If so, how well can they comprehend what is going on?
- ✓ Can my sunshine express their needs and understand what is happening?
- ✓ How will my sunshine child react to the hospital environment?
- ✓ Is there a comfortable, private room where the meeting can take place?
- ✓ What might my child feel when they see me in my current physical/emotional condition?
- ✓ What experience has my child had with death in the past and how is that impacting their current response?

3. Your Baby

The final thing you should consider is the physical condition of your baby.

- ✓ If your baby is expected to die shortly after birth: Does my care team think that the process of dying will be traumatic and therefore upsetting to my sunshine child or is it expected to be a peaceful process?

✓ Does my baby have any injuries, discoloration, or disfigurements that might upset my sunshine child?

Our experience was that Noemi was quite discolored from a lack of oxygen, as well as bruising from the medical team's attempts to resuscitate her. Additionally, her appearance quickly deteriorated after her death. As a result, we ultimately decided not to have our Sunshine meet Noemi because we felt that Noemi's body would have been startling and likely too frightening for our sunshine daughter.

In hindsight, I am still not sure that we made the best choice, but my husband and parents are confident we did. The important thing is that our decision did not seem to have a lasting impact on our sunshine child. She quickly understood her sister's death in a more profound way than I could ever have imagined such a small child would. I share this story of our family's uncertainty because the decisions around an infant's death can often feel extremely important and you can feel pressured to get everything right. However, with some distance, you realize that the impact of these decisions is ultimately much less significant than your commitment to accompany your sunshine child through their grief.

If You Decide to Have Your Child Meet or See the Baby

Parents who choose to have their sunshine children meet their sibling should take steps to prepare their child for this encounter. Talk openly and honestly about what the child will experience before the meeting happens. Think about what you can say to prepare them for:

✓ The baby's appearance
✓ Your appearance
✓ Other people who might be present in the room
✓ The room itself and any medical equipment that will be seen
✓ What they can do with the baby (hold, kiss, wash, dress etc.)
✓ Your emotions

✓ Rules and expectations for your child's behavior

For most children, seeing a very sick, dying, or dead person will be new and potentially frightening. You can reassure your sunshine child by explaining things to them in a calm, matter-of-fact way. Your explanations and comforting presence will remind your Sunshine that they can come to you with any questions that they need answered during the meeting.

You can also help your sunshine child by telling them how you expect them to act and what choices they may have ahead of time. For example, will they be able to hold the baby if they wish to? By preparing them for what they will do and how they should act, you help your sunshine child to know how to respond to this unfamiliar situation. This preparation also increases the likelihood that the meeting will be a positive one for your entire family.

During the meeting, be certain that you or another trusted adult is available for your sunshine child. Tell your sunshine child that you are available to discuss anything that they need to talk about. Provide reassurance that there are no right or wrong feelings in this situation. Similarly, make sure that they are empowered to do only what is comfortable for them.

As you witness this meeting, you will likely experience many powerful emotions of your own. It is always important to recognize and acknowledge your feelings. Once you have done that, however, try to think beyond your own emotions and imagine what is going on inside your sunshine child's head so that you can be present for them. Ask yourself:

✓ "What is my child thinking or feeling?"
✓ "How do they understand this?"
✓ "How did I respond to things that were very sad, scary, confusing or disappointing when I was their age?"
✓ "What does this mean to them?"

Use the answers to these questions to guide your own actions and responses to your child. This will help you to meet them where they are.

If You Decide Not to Have Your Child Meet or See the Baby

If you decide that a meeting between your Sunshine and the baby is not in the best interest of your family, there are still things that you can do to help your sunshine child comprehend the reality of the baby's death. Gathering physical reminders of your baby may be the most important way you can accomplish this. The tangible items you choose should symbolize the reality of their sibling's existence and also their death. The next chapter discusses ways to identify and collect these kinds of mementos for you and your sunshine child to treasure and share. By creating this memorial collection, you provide your sunshine child with tangible ways to get to know their sibling without ever meeting them. In my experience, having saved physical objects to share with my daughter was critical. These items helped my Sunshine grieve and feel included in our family's loss.

CHAPTER FOUR: SAVING MEMORIES

"You've changed me forever. And I'll never forget you."
-Kiera Cass

When a baby dies, families have a brief window of time to make memories of their cherished little one. In that short time, parents can gather items that will remind them of their child for years to come. As mentioned in the previous chapter, these objects will also help your sunshine child to get to know the baby while processing their grief. In fact, a survey of adults who lost their siblings during childhood found that siblings value the physical reminders that they have of their brothers' or sisters' lives.

In our family, this is certainly true. My Sunshine and I often sat together and riffled through our memory box of Noemi's "treasures." Even now, when my Sunshine sees me looking inside the box, she comes over to look with me. She sometimes uses these moments to ask me questions about her sister.

There are many ways to collect items that will remind you of your baby. Depending on where you delivered, the hospital may be able to assist. Many hospitals are quite knowledgeable about infant death and have procedures in place that help families gather reminders of their baby. Some provide special boxes, clothing, footprint kits and even photographers. Other hospitals may be less prepared for handling infant loss. At these hospitals, you may need to ask to keep various items that are meaningful to you. For example, I asked a nurse if I could keep the calendar pull-off for the day of my daughter's death. Table Two includes suggestions of things that you might want to gather and save.

In addition to collecting things that will help you remember your baby, you and your sunshine child can memorialize your infant through shared art projects. Since it is often difficult for children to express their emotions with language, working together on creative projects allows Sunshines to express their emotions while also providing you both with an opportunity to bond through your shared grief.

ITEMS TO HELP YOU REMEMBER YOUR BABY

THINGS TO KEEP

Photographs (Personal and Professional) [11]

The Baby's Blankets, Hats and Clothes [12]

Toys and Gifts the Baby Received

A Lock of Hair

Hand and Footprints

Items From a Baptism or Other Religious Ceremony

Flowers You Received

Sympathy Cards

Prayer Cards

THINGS TO MAKE

Letters to Your Baby

Scrapbooks or Photo Albums

Collages or Collage Boxes

Stories, Poems or Songs About the Baby

Hand Drawn Pictures or Paintings of the Baby

Flower Arrangements for the Cemetery or Funeral

Books About Your Baby or Family

Creative Displays of Treasured Objects

Christmas (or Other Holiday) Ornaments for the Baby

A Quilt Made from the Baby's Clothes or Blankets

CHAPTER FIVE: FUNERALS AND OTHER RITUALS OF GRIEF

"There are no goodbyes for us. Wherever you are, you will always be in my heart."
– Mahatma Gandhi

Rituals of grief, such as wakes and funerals, provide communities with an opportunity to support grieving families. In the recent past, American children were usually excluded from these rituals. This meant that they were unable to benefit from the community support that such events provide. Thankfully, child development specialists now understand that grief rituals are beneficial to children who choose to participate in them. In fact, the very act of participating in a loss ritual can help to build and solidify your child's support system. We witnessed this ourselves when our daughter bonded with the worship leader who sang at her sister's funeral. Over the next few years, this worship leader and his wife became a source of encouragement to our sunshine daughter.

In addition to the social benefits of participating in rituals surrounding death, these events can help sunshine children to understand death and give them an opportunity to express their emotions in a way that is safe and appropriate. Such rituals also offer a sense of closure and, while grief is only just beginning, they provide a sort of boundary between the days immediately following the baby's death and the months of healing that come afterwards.

Budgeting For Unexpected Ceremonies and Rituals

Organized grief rituals like funerals are beneficial, but they can also be cost prohibitive, particularly since an entire industry has been built around them. Families who lose a baby are often significantly impacted by the cost of these rituals since many of them have not set aside the necessary savings to cover the cost of a funeral. If having some sort of traditional grief ceremony is important to you but you are concerned about the cost, I encourage you to explore the options that are available to you. The following are things we learned that helped us to afford Noemi's funeral:

✓ Some funeral homes provide services for infants who have died free of charge, or they only charge for the costs that they incur.

✓ Houses of worship and religious leaders are often willing to waive fees or requested donations.

✓ Some cemeteries have sections that have been set aside for the burial of infants and offer their use for little or no cost to bereaved parents.

✓ Coffins, urns, and grave markers tend to come in a range of prices and it can be helpful to consider how much you are willing and able to spend on these before you begin to explore your choices.

✓ Families can often choose to forego, or they may wait to have one placed later.

✓ Some companies make relatively inexpensive grave markers for families that lose infants.

✓ Extended family is often eager to help and grief rituals provide them with the perfect opportunity to do so. For example, our family worked together to organize the service and reception when we were too overwhelmed to do so ourselves. They helped us by:

- Making memorial bookmarks/cards
- Setting and cleaning up
- Preparing refreshments
- Providing childcare for our Sunshine child while we were engaged in planning
- Reading requested verses and reflections
- Performing music

Their assistance was a huge gift to us because it meant that we could focus our energy on grieving Noemi and not on planning and financing her funeral. It also meant that we were deeply touched by the depth of their care and the many ways that our support community came together to help us through our grief. Their gifts of time and service continue to remind me of how much we are loved, even six years later.

While sunshine children can benefit from taking part in traditions surrounding the death of their siblings, it is critical that they only participate if they desire to do so. Parents should respect their sunshine child's preferences in this regard. Additionally, even children who choose to participate in a grief ritual may ultimately decide that it is too much for them to handle and it is important that parents communicate that this is okay. One way to do this is to have a designated adult (either a close friend or relative) who can stay near your child and accompany them if they need a break. For example, before Noemi's funeral, we told our sunshine daughter that she could go and play with her great-grandmother whenever she needed to leave. While she ended up staying with us throughout her sister's funeral service, knowing that she could escape helped her to relax and participate more fully. It also helped her father and I to focus without worrying about how to handle her behavior if she started to act like the energetic three-year-old that she was.

Because rituals of grief can play a key role in helping children to deal with their loss, preparation for these rituals is essential. Otherwise, they can be frightening and confusing to Sunshines. To prepare your sunshine child, you can tell them what to expect. For example, we had a Catholic Mass and burial service for Noemi, so in the days before the funeral, we told our sunshine daughter what we would be doing, what the burial would involve, and how we expected our daughter to behave during each part of our baby's funeral. We also made sure that our daughter knew that people would be very sad and the adults would probably cry. This was important because children may not be used to seeing adults express strong, negative emotions and we did not want our Sunshine to be unsettled by this.

You can prepare your child by talking with them about the following:

✓ Where will the ritual take place?
✓ Who will be participating/attending?
✓ What will it look like?
✓ What will people be doing?

✓ What expectations will there be for your sunshine child's behavior?

✓ What is the meaning behind the traditions?

✓ How long will it be?

✓ Will there be music? Readings? Speaking? Eating?

✓ What is a hearse?

✓ What is a coffin? Will it be open?

✓ What is cremation? What is an urn?

✓ What is a rabbi, minister, priest, or other officiant?

✓ What will happen to the baby's body after the funeral?

As you plan and prepare for these events, it can be helpful to know that there is often flexibility and room for personalizing the rituals. This can make it more meaningful for your sunshine child. For example, while a Catholic burial Mass is highly structured and has few options for making it more child friendly, we were able to choose the pieces of music that the organist would play during the Mass. We chose "Jesus Loves Me" as one of the songs at Noemi's funeral because this was a song that our young sunshine daughter had been singing to her sister during my pregnancy. Additionally, since I converted Catholicism as an adult, our priest worked closely with the Protestant minister who had been my youth pastor. They both participated in the service.

Another way we included our sunshine child in Noemi's funeral was by placing flowers on her grave as a family at the end of the service. Little acts of inclusion like these can make the difference between a sunshine child being a bored, lonely, forgotten observer and an active participant who shares in the emotional benefit of the ritual.

Due to the benefits of communal grief rituals, if your family does not belong to a community or religious group that participates in organized events surrounding death, your child may benefit from developing some grief rituals of your own. Grieving families have come up with many creative ways to honor their babies that are both spiritual and secular. Some have organized balloon releases.

Others have created memorial gardens or candle lighting ceremonies. Families have gathered loved ones to join for charitable walks or NICU book drives. These memorial events can be big or small depending on your family's preferences. The important thing is that they bring the people who support your family together so that your sunshine child can feel their embrace during this early time of grief.

Raising Sunshine

CHAPTER SIX: THE BABY'S STUFF

"You are braver than you believe, stronger than you seem and smarter than you think.
But the most important thing is, even if we are apart, I'll always be with you."
– A.A. Milne

At some point, you and your family will need to decide what to do with the items you have accumulated for your baby. All parents feel some sadness as they part with their child's clothes, toys, and other treasures when they are no longer needed. However, for grieving parents, this parting is often extremely painful. Letting go of your baby's "stuff" involves giving up some of the last physical reminders of your child and acknowledging the end of your hopes and dreams for the baby. This hard goodbye can feel like an impossible thing to do. Be gentle with yourself as you begin to face this process.

Grieving families do many different things with their baby's "stuff." Some leave their baby's nursery untouched, transforming it into a memorial. Others keep their infant's belongings safely stored away or save them with the thought that they might be needed for future children. Families may donate the baby's things to charity. Some families choose to sell or discard the baby's things. The music artist Prince took a decidedly dramatic approach: he had everything related to his son burned.[13]

Families need to do what feels best for them. Whenever possible, it is important to include sunshine children in decisions about their sibling's possessions, because this affects how sunshine children cope with their loss. The impact of this involvement was evident in a study that examined the experience of bereaved siblings.[14] Researchers found that those siblings who were not included in deciding what to do with the baby's possessions felt hurt and even "betrayed" by their parents. One participant in the study said, "My mom got rid of most of his clothes without telling me and I was just very, very upset." The last thing that our sunshine children need is to face more reasons to feel betrayed and upset.

Fortunately, when it comes to managing the baby's "stuff," maintaining good communication and making sure that sunshine children feel heard is all it takes to ensure that they feel included in the process.

Your sunshine child's age and temperament will determine how involved they can be in this process. For example, while we included our three-and-a-half-year-old daughter in some of our decisions, we made the decision to take apart Noemi's nursery on our own. In fact, my family cleared it out before I returned home from the hospital because I did not want to see her bedroom without her in it. Still, we made sure that our sunshine daughter was able to keep the things that were most important to her by making suggestions about what she might want to keep. We also chose to keep some of the things that she had made in anticipation of her baby sister's arrival.[15]

While older children may be capable of being more equal partners in the decision-making process, we found that it was helpful to give our young sunshine daughter specific options to choose between. If we had not done this, she would have kept everything (she is a bit of a pack rat even when she is not grieving). To avoid a situation in which our Sunshine wanted to keep everything, we told her up front that we would only keep things that were very special. In our case, our Sunshine chose to keep her sister's wall cling decorations and a framed ultrasound picture.

Talking about what will happen to the baby's belongings can also help sunshine children to let go of them. For example, as noted, we donated many of Noemi's things and our sunshine child had an easier time parting with these things when she knew that they would be used by babies in need. This helped her to feel like her loss had purpose.

If your sunshine child is older, they may be able to work collaboratively with you in making decisions about the baby's possessions. Older sunshine children often come up with great ideas about what you can do with the items. If your sunshine child has a heart for a particular charity, they might want to sell the items and donate the proceeds to that organization.

Throughout this process, it is important to remember that sunshine children of all ages associate certain objects with specific memories. This may mean that they want to keep an object, but it could also mean that it is too painful for them to have around. For example, when our Sunshine got older, she asked that we keep her sister's ultrasound picture someplace safe but hidden, because she wanted to keep it but she was sad every time she saw it. You can handle this by asking your child what objects are most important to them and letting them know that you can keep things stored away if that would make it easier for them.

Raising Sunshine

CHAPTER SEVEN: RETURNING TO LIFE

"...remembering does not preclude getting on with life."
– Katherine F. Donnelly

Although it might seem impossible right now, at some point you and your child will return to the world and your lives in it. While you will likely see that the world is largely unchanged, you and your sunshine child have changed significantly. As a result, returning to your daily lives can feel unsettling and disorienting. For Sunshines, it can even be frightening. It may be difficult for your sunshine child to imagine doing the things that you used to do or spending time with people who will ask about the baby. It is vital to prepare for their re-entry into life outside of your family unit.

When to Start Reintegrating

Each family reintegrates into their daily lives differently. Some choose to return to their routines as quickly as possible. Others need time off from the burdens of daily life so that they can be together as they grieve and find comfort in a safe place. Even within a family, individual members may approach re-entry differently. In my family, I took the longest to settle back into a daily routine.

Talking with your sunshine child can help you plan for this reentry. Children (particularly young children) benefit from returning to predictable routines as quickly as possible and are often eager to do so. For them, attending school and resuming normal activities restores a sense of control and mastery over life. It also offers them a reprieve from witnessing your grief which can be scary and upsetting to them. When our sunshine daughter started doing normal little kid stuff outside of our home, I quickly realized that these were necessary mini vacations from her grief.

Still, some sunshine children need time to process their grief before getting back into a routine. They might need time to express and process their emotions in a safe place or they may just need to be reassured by being close to you. Many sunshine children are afraid to separate from their parents after a tragedy like sibling death because they realize that if their sibling could die, their parents could also die. In fact, one study of bereaved siblings found that they were more concerned about death than the average population.

If your sunshine child is anxious about separating from you, respecting their need to be extra close to you for a little while may help to avoid difficulties in the future. Once things settle down and your child feels more secure, they will likely be ready to leave you for periods of time. If you have to separate from your sunshine child or if your sunshine child's separation anxiety continues after the initial shock of their grief, there are things that you can do to help, such as:

Talk with your sunshine child

Talking with and listening to your sunshine child makes everything better. When you listen carefully to what they are thinking and feeling, you are better able to help them problem solve, provide them with support, and let them know how deeply you care about them. Just the simple act of being available to them can make the difference between your sunshine child feeling all alone and feeling safe and supported enough to do the things they fear most.

Remind yourself that your sunshine child is resilient

It is worth remembering that children can bounce back from very difficult situations. This can help you to stay calm and present for your sunshine child so that you can help them to build the skills they need to become even more resilient. Whenever I worry about my Sunshine's ability to weather life's storms, I think about my father-in-law who, as a young child witnessed the horror of Nazis storming his city. Only six years later, he found himself filled with foreboding when the Red Army "liberated" that same city. In spite of these traumas, he grew to be a kind, successful and wonderful man who raised a family who loves him deeply. It is worth considering the stories of resilience you have in your own family history. So many families have tales of incredible courage and adaptability that can provide hope to us as we face our own trials.

Stay calm and positive when you leave

Children take cues from their parents' emotions. If you remain calm when facing challenges, your sunshine child is less likely to feel anxious. On the other hand, if you are nervous and worried about your child being away from you, they will pick up on this and assume that there must be a good reason to feel anxious. By managing your own emotions, you might not eliminate your sunshine child's separation anxiety, but you will avoid adding to it.

Keep your goodbye quick and predictable

Have a short goodbye routine (like "kissing hands" or a quick hug). Follow your routine whenever you separate from your sunshine. In our family, we kiss our palm and then press our hands together, transferring a kiss that we will carry throughout the day.

Practice being apart

Practice being apart at times when your sunshine child is calm, refreshed, and happy. At first, you may only be able to do this for a few minutes or by moving into a different part of the house. Eventually, you can stay away for longer periods of time. By doing this, you allow your child to develop the self-soothing skills and confidence they need to be away from you for longer periods of time.

Provide clear expectations and always follow through

Your sunshine child will feel more secure if you tell them when they can expect you to return. Of course, many children, do not understand time so you may need to say something like, "I will be back after snack time." Tell your sunshine child who they will be with and what they will be doing while you are gone. Then make sure that you return as promised so that they build trust in your promises.

Let your child make a choice

Most children calm down as soon as they become engaged in an activity. You can help to distract your sunshine child and simultaneously give them the sense that they have some control over their situation by offering them choices. For example, you might ask, "Do you want to join the kids at the sand table or the kids playing with blocks?"

Give your child an attachment object

If your child has an attachment object, whether a picture or stuffed "lovey," these can be very helpful during transition times. Even older children may feel more confident if they carry a picture of you in their backpack or pocket. Research suggests that people of all ages experience a wave of positive emotions when they look at the face of a loved one. The great news is that looking at an image of a beloved face has the same positive effect as seeing the person, so a picture of your face can help your child to feel reassured even when you are not actually present. Another way to ease separation is to write your child a brief note saying, "I love you!" and hide it in their lunch box. Little reminders that you are loving them from wherever you are can be reassuring to a struggling child.

Preparing Your Sunshine Child to Reintegrate

As you and your sunshine child prepare to resume your daily lives again, you will likely both experience some anxiety about what re-engagement will look like. On the other hand, you might assume that reintegration will be easy and then be surprised when challenges come along. The good news is that there are steps you can take to help make the transition to your "new normal" as smooth as possible.

Talk with your sunshine child

Yes, it's the same old suggestion again, but it is really so important. Talk with your sunshine child about what you both expect returning to daily life will look like and share any concerns that you may have. You can then fill in any gaps that your sunshine child has in their expectations so that they are better prepared for what will happen. Help them to think about what to expect in all areas of reintegration including schoolwork, teachers, friends, extra-curricular activities, emotions, and energy levels. Listen to your child's concerns and brainstorm ways that you can address them together.

Figure out who needs to know

If your sunshine child is young, it will be important that you let their caregivers know about the baby's death. This will prepare other adults to help your child while giving them a chance to consider how to address the death with the other children that your child interacts with. Since young children may struggle to share their experiences, they rely on you to convey this information to the people around them. For very young children, this might happen more naturally because parents tend to interact more frequently with daycare providers. Parents of preschoolers and young grade school students might need to intentionally reach out to their child's teacher.

If your sunshine child is older, you should ask if they want you to tell their teachers about the baby's death. You can discuss how doing so could be helpful to their teachers and might give them a chance to prepare the other students for your child's return. However, if your older sunshine child would rather their teachers not know what happened, it is important to respect this. Some older children see out-of-home activities as places where they can be "normal" – a respite from the grief that they have been living with. Others do not want to seem different from their peers in any way. The importance for older sunshine children to have a level of control over their own privacy cannot be overstated.

Sample Roleplay

You: Is there a particular part of going back to school that makes you nervous?

Child: I just don't know what to say. I'm afraid it will be just like the funeral and everyone will be looking at me and saying they are sorry and I hate that.

You: Hmm. Maybe we can think about what you could say if that happens. Do you have any thoughts?

Child: Well, I want to say, "STOP BRINGING IT UP!" and "STOP LOOKING AT ME!" but I can't.

You: I get that. When that happens to me, I try to remember that they are saying that because they are concerned and probably don't know what else to say. I suspect they feel uncomfortable, too. Sometimes, I say something like, "Thank you. I don't really feel like talking about it and I want to think about something else for a while, but it makes me feel good to know you care about me." Do you think maybe you could say something like that?

Child: Hmm...I don't, know...I guess that might work. I could say, "I want to do something else right now but thank you for thinking about me."

You: That sounds great. Do you want to practice saying it a few times together?

Child: Ok.

You: How about I be your friend from school and you can be yourself. Okay, here we go: 'I heard about your brother! I am so sorry!'

Child: I don't really want to talk about it right now but thanks for thinking about me. Why don't we play on the playground?

You: Sure! Wanna play tag?

Roleplay social situations

While sunshine children are often eager to return to school and be with their friends, they may be unsure of how to handle talking about their loss with their friends and teachers. They may want to share the experience of their sibling's death, and many bereaved siblings feel intuitively that it is helpful to do so. Still, it can be difficult for them to know how to raise the subject. You can help them prepare by acting out conversations so that they can practice what to say. [16]

Before you begin role-playing, talk with your child about the specific things that they are anxious about so that you can target these together.

Being a Family Again

While work and school take up most of our waking lives, reintegrating into daily life happens in many other settings. It involves finding ways to reconnect and have fun as a family again. Too often, grieving families feel guilty when they have a good time. This guilt can prevent them from truly living. If you and your sunshine child feel badly about enjoying life after your baby's death, remind yourselves that you both deserve to be happy. You were made for all of life - its sorrows and its joys – and your life did not end when the baby's did.

It can be hard to force yourself beyond your pain and into joy again. In my own experience, I was able to muster the motivation to do this by remembering three things:

- ✓ Noemi would have loved me and because of that she would delight in my happiness. After all, when we love someone, we want them to be happy.
- ✓ My Sunshine deserves to live her own, meaningful life. She needs my help to do that and one of the ways that I can help her is by ushering joy, happiness, and laughter into our home again.
- ✓ I already had one child torn from my life. I did not want my grief to steal my enjoyment of the treasured child that I had left.

I encourage you to make fun a priority in your home for the same three reasons that I did. At first, this will take a lot of conscious thought and effort. For a while, having fun will probably be the most exhausting thing on your to-do list. It will not come easily, and it may only last briefly, but it will be easier and last longer as time goes on. As you work to incorporate joy into your home again, know that when you see your sunshine child's smile return, it will be worth all of your effort.

Tips to Kickstart Family Fun

- ✓ Explore someplace you've never been
- ✓ Attend a concert, play or sporting event
- ✓ Visit friends
- ✓ Make and fly a kite
- ✓ Go on a scavenger hunt
- ✓ Have a boardgame tournament
- ✓ Make popcorn and watch a tried-and-true comedy
- ✓ Host a family sing-a-long movie night
- ✓ Go to a museum
- ✓ Plant a garden together
- ✓ Go to the beach
- ✓ Have a whipped cream or snowball fight
- ✓ Play hide-and-seek
- ✓ Swing in a hammock
- ✓ Get a new pet

As I write this, I am reminded of the moment when I knew that my family would not dwell in the darkness of grief forever. The three of us took a day trip to a cranberry festival on Cape Cod. It was warm but not too hot – just right for a New England fall day. The sounds and smells of a fair surrounded us, and we were lost in a crowd of people who were celebrating another harvest. My Sunshine was fascinated by the way that cranberries grow and by the machines that are used to harvest them. She was thrilled to have the opportunity to grow a cranberry plant of her own. Mostly, she was ecstatic about riding on a school bus for the first time. As I sat with her, bumping along on the bus and bracing my still sore c-section wound, I looked at her small, enthralled face and felt something that I had forgotten: happiness. It was fleeting and fragile, but it was there. In that moment, I knew that we would survive our loss because the world still held much beauty and goodness. But I also knew that we would be okay because I vowed not to let the pain of loss blind us to the little miracles that surround us every day.

Raising Sunshine

SECTION II: SELF-CARE FOR PARENTS

"The mindset of a loss of a loved one is to understand that the loss will never be undone. You must live with it, like it or not. But, to live well, you must turn that loss into something positive. That way, you can become the best version of yourself; scarred, flawed and unstoppable."
– Val Uchendu

"It is human to have your soul brought to a crisis you did not anticipate."
– The Dune Series

Grieving parents are not superheroes with infinite strength, energy and emotional reserves. As a result, their grief will inevitably impact their families in many ways. In fact, one researcher wrote, "The parents' management of their own grief and construction of the meaning of the loss has an enormous impact on surviving children." Whether we wish it to or not, our grief will play a significant role in how our sunshine children weather their sibling's death. So, we have a choice to make. We can surrender to our grief and become the parents that Katherine Donnelly described when she wrote, "Parents who are bleeding emotionally are often simply unable to help the surviving children during the first months and even years." Or we can choose to take care of ourselves so that we can be parents that are dependably present supports for our Sunshines. The choice is really ours.[17]

For me, this decision was a simple one. Early in my grief, I read multiple research articles about grieving siblings who felt unloved and abandoned by their sorrowful parents. I knew that I did not want that for my Sunshine and, while I could not shelter her from the realities of grief, I could ensure that I walked with her through it.

Additionally, as I alluded to in the previous chapter, there was no way that I was going to allow Noemi's illness and death to rob me of my opportunity to parent my first-born daughter. I was determined to be the parent my Sunshine needed when she needed me the most and it was this resolve that drove me back into the land of the living. I had to heal emotionally because my living daughter needed me. In a way, while I was struggling to help her, she was saving me.

Even early on, I sensed that I would never be the person or mother that I was before Noemi died. However, I was committed to doing whatever was needed to heal the wounds of my loss so that I could fully participate in my sunshine daughter's life. This required allowing myself the space for self-care while I juggled the demands of grief and parenting. This second section of the book was written to encourage you to do the same.

As someone who has experienced the incredible pain of infant loss myself, my deepest hope for this book is that it provides information and comfort to all of its readers. As I prepared for publication, I became aware that not all parents who grieve identify themselves by the traditional terms used for parents. LGBTQ+ families, for example, may use different titles to express their relationships to their babies. For the purposes of this book, I have chosen to use the traditional terms of mother and father for simplicity. However, if these titles are upsetting to you or make it difficult for you to access the information that I am providing, please reach out to me at sroubek.ariane@gmail.com and I will be happy to send you a complementary version of Section II that uses non-gendered language.

CHAPTER EIGHT: SELF-CARE FOR ALL PARENTS

"The strongest woman in the world is the grieving mother that wakes up and keeps going every morning."
- Tara Watkins Anderson

"It takes a strong man to be a father and an even stronger man to be a grieving father."
- Unknown

You have probably already realized that the death of a child is unlike any other loss that families face. The physical and emotional toll it takes is heavy and at times seems unrelenting. In fact, scientists have observed that the sorrow that parents feel for a deceased child is more powerful, lasting, and complex than any other kind of grief. While it can be overwhelming to parent your sunshine child while you are wrestling with such all-consuming sadness, it is essential that you find a way to do so.

How you manage your grief is critical to your sunshine child's ability to survive and, ultimately, thrive. In your child's eyes, you are as close as it comes to a living, breathing superhero, and while you will not always live up to this perception, your desire and determination to parent your sunshine child as you grieve is truly heroic. However, even superheroes must protect their superpowers, and that is why taking care of yourself is so important.

To start, focus on the basics of healthy living so that you can build a solid foundation of self-care. These include:

- ✓ Eat nutritious foods
- ✓ Drink a lot of fluids to stay hydrated
- ✓ Keep up with your prescribed medications
- ✓ Get enough sleep and rest
- ✓ Exercise (even if it is just a walk around the block)

- ✓ Do not drive or use heavy machines unless you are medically cleared to do so, are well rested, and are not taking any medications that could cause you to be groggy
- ✓ Minimize alcohol consumption and avoid other substances
- ✓ Take time to be alone, but also spend time with friends
- ✓ Do things that bring you pleasure (scheduling these into your calendar if you must)

You may find it to be challenging to do these things for yourself while your family is struggling to heal from the physical and emotional toll of your baby's death. If you are having trouble focusing on your own needs, use the Daily Self-Care To-Do List in Appendix I to help you stay on track. If juggling everything feels overwhelming, brainstorm ways that you can get the assistance you need to prioritize your own wellbeing. For example, you might consider:

- ✓ Asking your partner or other family members to take over your caregiving responsibilities for an hour or two
- ✓ Delegating household tasks to friends or family who have offered to help
- ✓ Accept help from your community
- ✓ Whenever possible, reducing your usual responsibilities by eating out more often, using a grocery delivery service or hiring someone to clean the house for a while
- ✓ Using vacation time or an FMLA leave so that you don't have to worry about work on top of everything else

There are many ways to get the support that you need so that you can prioritize your own health. While some of them come at a cost, many options will not break your budget. For example, ordering groceries from a delivery service actually saved us money because we did not buy things impulsively.

Psychology Nerd Moment: Bettelheim and Winnicott

Dr. Bruno Bettelheim and Dr. Donald Winnicott gave the world a revolutionary piece of parenting advice when they suggested that parents only need to be "good enough." Their advice is to be intentional about not seeking perfection. They recognized that mistakes are inevitable and parents have limited time, energy, and ability to give of themselves. Rather than developing a formula to overcome these realities, Drs. Bettelheim and Winnicott suggested that children do not need perfect parents – in fact, they are better off without them! Bettelheim realized that parents who struggled for perfection end up hurting their children more than helping them. Consequently, he described the ideal "good enough" parent as someone who:

- is okay with imperfection
- is respectful of their child
- seeks to understand their child and the way that they view the world
- let's their child be a kid and doesn't worry about the future
- offers help only when their child asks for it
            AND
- takes on the responsibilities of being an adult so that their child feels provided for and protected

That's it! Two of the most influential guys in the history of Child Psychology declared that if

- your laundry piles rival Everest
- your kid's daycare friends notice that all you ever send for lunch is frozen chicken nuggets
- you are late for everything
- you let your kids occupy themselves for hours without offering guided activities

- your sunshine child's clothes do not match
- you do not plan a Pinterest worthy birthday party or greet your kid with homemade chocolate chip cookies every day after school
- you limit your kids' afterschool activities to one per child
- breakfast for dinner is more common than dinner for dinner

AND

- your kids run around outside in diapers, bare feet, and layers of mud[18]

...you can still be the ideal parent for your Sunshine. I am not suggesting that you should give your kids junk food exclusively, or that having a well-ordered home is not something worth striving for. However, I hope that you can take comfort in knowing that you have a lot of leeway to give yourself some grace during this particularly challenging season. In other words, your laundry and housework can wait because, if at the end of the day you and your family are all fed, safe, washed, supported, and loved, then you have conquered!

Once you have decided to prioritize your wellbeing, the next step is to embrace the idea of being "good enough." Everywhere you look, you will find advice about how to parent: online, in magazines, from teachers, on TV, even in this book! Some of the parenting advice offered is based on research and easy to follow. Other suggestions are flawed or unrealistic. The truth is, your Sunshine doesn't need a perfect parent. Instead, they need a parent who loves them and who is emotionally available to them. To be that parent to them, you are going to have to let some things go so that you can focus on self-care.

CHAPTER NINE: BUILDING YOUR TEAM

"A best friend is the only one who walks into your life when the world has walked out."
– Shannon L. Alder

We have all watched the drama play out on television: a child dies and the parents' marriage falls apart as a result. For years, society has assumed that child loss and parental discord inevitably go hand in hand. In fact, my husband and I just watched a movie in which one of the main characters says, "No marriage can survive the death of a child." The fact is, however, that the assumption that child loss will inevitably lead to troubled marriages is not based in fact. Unfortunately, regardless of how inaccurate it may be, it can create a lot of anxiety for grieving parents who fear the secondary loss of losing their partners in the wake of their child's death.

When my daughter died, I worried that my marriage would suffer because of our loss. This terrified me because I did not think that I could survive the end of my marriage on top of the grief that I was already feeling. However, both my husband and I approach our marriage with the conviction that our marriage is for life and there are no emergency exits. This commitment made me hope that relationship difficulties were not an inevitable result of infant loss. When I began to research how child death impacts parental relationships, I discovered that the truth was both reassuring and provided motivation to fight for my marriage.

Studies have found that, while a child's death certainly influences the parental relationships, the true impact of the death varies. While a few studies note that between eighty and ninety percent of parents who lose a child get divorced, many other studies indicate that the rates are much lower. For example, a large survey of parents found that seventy-two percent of couples remained married after their child's death. Additionally, of the twenty-eight percent of couples who were no longer married by the time of the study, only a portion of these marriages ended because of divorce (others ended when one or both spouses died). Considering that roughly half of all marriages in the United States currently end in divorce, this latter study suggests that the odds of staying married after the death of a child are quite good. Even if the true divorce rate for bereaved couples was underestimated by this study, the data clearly shows that not all grieving parents are destined for divorce.

Another study, performed in the 1990s, followed couples for six months after their baby's death. The researchers found that in the first months after their loss, some marriages did break-up. However, after the first six months had passed, parents whose babies died were no more likely to experience relationship conflict than those whose infants lived. These findings suggest that, while infant loss may be a contributing factor to marital conflict, it does not invariably lead to the end of significant relationships. In fact, studies that focus on the quality of relationships, rather than their survival, have found better news: up to a quarter of marriage relationships become closer after the loss of a child. [19]

Despite my early fears, my marriage was one of those that grew stronger after Noemi died. Our shared experience of loss, care for one another, and commitment to each other - regardless of our circumstances - helped our love grow deeper and stronger. My husband and I were both changed by Noemi's death, but we changed together and became more united in our purpose as a couple. In fact, the loss of our daughter was one of the most defining moments of our marriage so far and it moved us from the tentative post-honeymoon days into a deeper, more mature relationship that has been tried, tested, and survived.

While, the death of a child does not necessarily result in a doomed relationship, it is important to keep in mind that whatever impact infant loss does have on your relationship with your partner will impact your sunshine children. Children whose parents are frequently in conflict are more likely to experience:

✓ Increased levels of stress
✓ Feelings of helplessness

- ✓ Emotional difficulties
- ✓ Behavioral problems
- ✓ Social challenges
- ✓ Academic struggles

Psychology Nerd Moment: ACEs, Protective Factors, and Your Relationship

When psychologists think about the impact of childhood trauma, they often consider Adverse Childhood Experiences (ACEs). ACEs are problems that children encounter which make them more likely to face a variety of physical and mental challenges throughout their lives. The more ACEs a child experiences, the more likely they are to experience future difficulties. Your sunshine child has experienced at least one ACE: the death of their sibling.

While it can be upsetting to know that this loss may make them more vulnerable to challenges, the good news is that there are "protective factors" that limit the impact that ACEs have on our children. The more protective factors a child has, the less likely it is that ACEs will have a long-term impact on the child's life.

There are things you can do right now to build protective factors for your child. Amazingly, by prioritizing your relationship with your partner, you are strengthening two important ones:

1. You are helping to create and maintain a safe, stable, and consistent family relationship for your sunshine child
2. You are ensuring that your child has parents that strive to resolve conflicts peacefully and effectively, thus limiting their exposure to parental arguments

---

Additionally, when parents argue, children feel less secure within their families. This is particularly problematic for our sunshine kids, who were already shaken by their sibling's death. Thus, protecting and strengthening the relationship with your partner should be prioritized because this benefits both you and your sunshine child.[20]

Your relationship with your partner impacts your sunshine child in many ways, so when you prioritize your relationship, you help your sunshine child. Of course, when the dazzling glow of new love has faded and you find yourselves standing together in the middle of stark and sometimes brutal realities, kindling your love can be difficult. I have found that the following six action steps can encourage you to grow together as you weather this storm:

1. **Support One Another**

   There is a Bible verse that says, "Though one may be overpowered, two can defend themselves. A cord of three strands is not quickly broken." (Ecclesiastes 4:12). This verse is a popular one to read at weddings because it reminds us that we are stronger together than we are individually. When we imagine a cord that is a single strand, we can see that it has areas of weakness that are vulnerable and may break under stress. However, if we picture that same single strand being woven with other strands, we find that the strands within the woven cord combine to strengthen each other's areas of weakness. In the same way, our relationship with our partner gives us the opportunity to be strong when they are not and to find support in our own areas of weakness.

   This is particularly true in the aftermath of infant loss. Both partners bear the weight of grief together, but the way that they process this grief is different. Therefore, when one is overwhelmed, the other often remains resilient and when one struggles to express their emotions, the other may help them to give their feelings a voice. Consequently, by grieving together - but differently - parents are better able to survive the loss of their baby.

   This was certainly true in our family. My world halted for a while when Noemi died and if it had been just me, our family would have stopped functioning. We would have had no income, no food, and no routine. My husband, however, found solace in getting life back to normal and, sometimes singlehandedly, kept our family going. Perhaps because of his need to carry on, however, he found it difficult to articulate his grief and accept support. My own ability to explore and express emotion and my eagerness to incorporate rituals of grief into our daily life encouraged him to find a place for his sorrow in our busy lives. Left alone, each of us would likely have broken but, because we grieved together, we were able to navigate Noemi's death and its aftermath.

There are many ways that you and your partner can support each other as you grieve, and these are rooted in your own unique personalities and relationship dynamics. Some ideas that you can use to help you think of ways to support your partner include:

- ✓ Paying attention to what your partner needs and figuring out how to meet that need
- ✓ Sending "I love you" texts or leaving love notes in your partner's work bag
- ✓ Checking in on your partner throughout the day
- ✓ Giving your partner flowers, special snacks, or other little gifts to show your love
- ✓ Working together to ensure that physical needs, such as sleep and exercise, are met
- ✓ Finding ways to help your partner identify and address their emotions
- ✓ Actively sharing the parenting of your sunshine child

Whatever your support looks like, it will reinforce your unity as a team. Conflict and difficulties are inescapable parts of any partnership, but your commitment to working together and your support for one another will help you both to heal.

2. Communicate Well

There are many self-help books for couples that focus on communicating more effectively. These can be worth reading because the lessons that they contain are especially important during times of stress and sorrow. Unfortunately, simply reading a manual will not transform you into a great communicator. Still, there are some things you can do to improve your communication even before you look at a relationship book:

✓ Focus on your partner

Find time when you can be together without distractions so that you can listen carefully to what your partner is saying. Then take time to think about how you want to respond. As you listen, show your partner that you are paying attention to them by using body language. Lean toward them, look at them, make eye-contact when appropriate, and touch them. By doing this, you convey that you are physically and mentally present and available to your spouse.

✓ Be an active listener

Don't just listen to what your partner is saying - engage with it. If you don't understand something, ask open ended questions such as, "What was it like for you to talk with our sunshine child about the baby's death?" Clarify what you think you understand by asking, "I think you are telling me that you are feeling _____. Is that right?" Once you are confident that you understand what your partner is communicating, think about how you can relate to their thoughts and feelings. Build on what your partner says rather than jumping to a completely different topic or steering the conversation toward something that you are more comfortable with.

✓ **Do not play the blame game**

When problems arise, convey your emotions without making accusations. For example, instead of saying "How could you do that? You don't care about me at all!" say something like, "I was angry when I saw that you posted that online without asking me. I wasn't ready to share that information and I feel embarrassed and worried about what people will think about us." This allows your partner to understand why you are upset without becoming defensive and feeling attacked. Rather than starting a battle, you are encouraging a meaningful conversation and asking your partner to work with you to fix the problem and avoid its repetition in the future.

✓ **Be honest about your feelings**

Many grieving couples experience a range of negative emotions and it can be tempting to hide or avoid them. However, it is important that you work through feelings like isolation, guilt, blame and diminished sex drives together. By doing so, you avoid building walls around your emotions that can push you and your partner apart. You also give each other the opportunity to care for one another in the areas that most need care. Remember, your goal is to be like strands of a cord wrapped together and compensating for one another's weaknesses, not a solitary rod of titanium.

✓ **Be kind**

While you should be honest, choose your words carefully so that they do not wound your partner. John Gottman (who is arguably the most important relationship researcher of our time) concluded that, "The people who have stable, happy relationships are much gentler with one another than people who have unhappy relationships or break up." In other words, things like name calling, swearing, walking away, exasperated gestures, and sarcasm should be avoided during a confrontation. Instead, you should focus on communicating your feelings and needs gently and without attacking your spouse. For example, you might say, "It hurt when you yelled at me. I do not know what I did to upset you. I know you are stressed, and I want to help you, but I do not want you to talk to me like that in the future." View your disagreements as opportunities to strengthen and improve your relationship, rather than seeing them as competitions to be won.

Psychology Nerd Moment: John Gottman

John Gottman's research into relationships is fascinating. A lot of his work involved analyzing video tapes of relationships to find micro-expressions which are fleeting movements we make with our faces that reveal our true emotions. By using this data, he was able to predict which emotions are most associated with strong marital relationships and which tend to lead to divorce.

---

3. **Respect Differences**
As we have discussed, people grieve differently. You may find that one of you grieves more intensely and longer while the other one recovers more quickly. Or one of you might feel the need to share your experience with everyone you meet while the other does not talk about it at all. If you give each other the respect and space to grieve freely, you will likely find that you and your partner are drawn closer together through your

grief, even though your experiences of it are very different. Remember, it is precisely because you grieve differently that you can help one another when one of you is struggling.

Similarly, it is important that you respect the ways that your partner is changed by your baby's death. No one escapes from child-loss unchanged. In the wake of infant loss, many parents reevaluate their priorities, discover new strengths, and explore new interests. They grow into people who are different from the ones they were before they lost their baby. These changes can be hard to tolerate in someone you love, but it is necessary to do so because it is the only way that you can grow together.

In my own marriage, we often categorize different events in our life as happening "before Noemi" or "after Noemi." It is as if our shared understanding that Noemi's death changed us in profound ways provides us with the framework to organize our experiences into those we had before and after her death. Although we are not the same people we were when we made our wedding vows, our love for each other is stronger because it was able to expand and embrace the people we are today. We think more deeply and intentionally about many things. This can be helpful, but it can also be colored by our lost naivete which causes us to be less optimistic. But we are also stronger and simultaneously more independent and inter-dependent. We have also learned to be more vulnerable. Together, we have grown in our compassion for others and we continue to grow in our ability to let go of our need for control and accept what life brings. Most importantly, we love each other more richly and deeply.

4. Enjoy Each Other

You cannot appreciate the ways that your partner is changed by grief if you do not spend time to get to know the person they are becoming. Ask yourself:

If you had never done anything fun with your partner when you first met, would you have ended up together?

I suspect that you probably would not have, because most relationships are built in low-pressure, enjoyable environments. More than likely, you dated and spent time getting to know each other and this relationship building "work" helped you connect.

The importance of time spent alone together does not end when you become parents. Research that looked at "date nights" for married couples found that those who continued to "date" one another after marriage had better communication and an increased sense of togetherness. In addition, they reported feeling less stressed overall. Not surprisingly, the couples that spent more time alone with one another had lower rates of divorce than those that had little one-on-one time. When married couples dated intentionally, they felt a renewed sense of romance and they continued to view their partner as exciting long after the glow of new love had faded. Another study found that couples who went on interesting dates were more satisfied and reported less boredom with their partner. [21]

Date Night Ideas

✓ Go for a hike
✓ Investigate a new neighborhood
✓ Explore a museum
✓ Attend a concert or theatrical performance

- ✓ Try a new ethnic food
- ✓ Journey to somewhere you have never explored (it doesn't have to be far away)
- ✓ Participate in a mail-order or theatrical mystery
- ✓ Take a class (photography, cooking, glass blowing, gardening, stargazing - the options are endless)
- ✓ Take a bike ride
- ✓ Go kayaking or canoeing
- ✓ Find a local festival to experience
- ✓ Look up interesting local history and set out on a self-guided tour of the sites where these events happened
- ✓ Go mini-golfing or bowling
- ✓ Take a fitness class
- ✓ Volunteer together
- ✓ Find a park near you and have an outdoor adventure
- ✓ Find your way out of an escape room
- ✓ Go on a tour
- ✓ Build something together
- ✓ Plan a DIY paint night
- ✓ Pack a picnic and watch the sunset or sunrise
- ✓ Train for a road race together

As you face the stress that grief puts on your relationship, it is particularly important that you carve out time to spend with your partner, getting to know who they are becoming as they grow and change through loss. However, the weight of grief can make everything feel serious and heavy, and it can be difficult to put effort into maintaining your relationship when you are using all your energy just to survive. For this reason, I offer some ideas to take the work out of date night planning in the table entitled, *Date Night Ideas.*

When you push yourself to prioritize time with your partner, you will be reminded of who you fell in love with. One-on-one activities will help you to develop appreciation and deep caring for one another, which researcher John Gottman says is the key to a lasting relationship. He has found that, "What makes love last is cherishing your partner and feeling lucky that you have this person in your life. The act of cherishing is something that some couples build."

5. Be Patient

It takes time to heal from the loss of a child. Eventually, your lives will become less consumed by your grief, but even then, you may continue to dwell on your loss for a long time. Additionally, many couples find that one partner heals more quickly than the other since everyone processes their grief differently. When a couple is out-of-sync, both partners face the challenge of being patient with one another. It is understandably frustrating to be dragged down by someone whose profound sadness is prolonged. At the same time, it is confusing and upsetting to see someone move on from grief if you are still consumed by it. Only your patience and willingness to view your partner without judgment will allow you to support one another through this time. Unfortunately, you are at a disadvantage because grief related stress can make couples short tempered in their daily lives, so it is important that you are aware of your reactions to your spouse and monitor negative emotions like frustration.

The best advice that I can give is not to expect perfection from each other during this time. Your grief will reveal some of the worst parts of yourselves and you will both have to grapple with these. However, you will also discover how courageous you are as you live each day with the weight of your loss bearing down. In time, you will discover one another's greatest strengths and watch as your child's death forges these into great gifts for one another. You will also discover how deep the love you share is as you witness it survive through sorrow.

As you live each day together, pay attention to the ways that your grief is revealing the best in your partner. It will be easier to extend grace to each other knowing that, while it will take time to feel anything like "normal," the wait will be worthwhile. On those days when the worst aspects of your partner are all you can see, the sentiments of the Serenity Prayer can help you keep pushing on:

> *"God, grant me the serenity to accept the things I cannot change..."*

6. Do not wait to make a change[22]

Many times, relationship problems result from a failure to connect with one another in a meaningful way. Whether it is because of laziness, busyness, or as a defense against past hurts, this disconnect leaves you feeling less compassion and love for your partner. However, psychological research shows that changed behaviors can lead to changed emotions. Consequently, when partners feel disconnected and distant, their relationship can be healed when one partner tries to rekindle the relationship.

Rather than waiting for your partner to initiate changes in your relationship, do it yourself. Take responsibility for your relationship by initiating change. Start by doing little things each day to help your partner and to let them know that they are loved. Instead of letting time pass while you wait for them to love you better, focus on what you can do to demonstrate your love for them right now. Even if you do not feel particularly loving toward your partner, "fake it 'til you make it." Over time, this shift in your focus and actions will change the dynamics of your relationship, making it a more loving and positive haven for both of you.

At the same time, it will enrich your understanding of love. Too often, we think of love as a feeling, but emotions are fleeting and if that is all love is, then our relationships will be as transient as sifting piles of sand. Real, lasting love is much more than an emotion: it is a commitment to keep acting in the best interest of the one we choose to love, even when we do not feel particularly loving. When you keep doing things in love even though you do not have an emotional desire to do so you are building the deepest, most enduring type of love there is.

7. Seek Intimacy

Healthy partnerships promote intimacy on two levels: emotional and physical. We have already addressed the importance of time alone and of talking openly about your thoughts and feelings. By doing this, you establish emotional intimacy.

Physical intimacy after the loss of a baby is also important for partners. Of course, like most activities after infant loss, being physically intimate can be complicated. Studies have found that couples who are sexually active soon after their loss tend to grieve less intensely and for a shorter amount of time. Unfortunately, it can be difficult to rekindle your sexual relationship after your baby dies.

Many parents who give birth are not able to engage in sexual intercourse until they recover from the pregnancy and delivery. Some need to wait until they can secure birth control so that they can avoid an unplanned and potentially dangerous pregnancy. Fortunately, sexual intercourse is not the only way to be physically intimate during this time. Since touch and closeness are often soothing, it is worth focusing on alternative ways to be intimate soon after your loss. As one bereaved father wrote, "In the early days a hug meant a lot. It made me feel close to her without having sex."

In my own marriage, I was surprised by how comforting it was to simply touch my husband. When I had trouble falling asleep because my mind was full of my baby, simply laying my hand on his back helped me to relax enough to sleep.

Another reason to maintain physical contact even when you are not able to be sexually active is that such touch makes it easier to eventually resume sexual intercourse. Sands, an organization that is dedicated to helping families through the loss of an infant, suggests that couples who struggle to maintain physical contact find it helpful to set goals for themselves so that they continue to be physically close. Some examples of such goals are:

- ✓ Hug twice a day
- ✓ Kiss every morning
- ✓ Hold hands while watching TV
- ✓ Lie close to each other in bed
- ✓ Give a massage every-other-day
- ✓ Shower together weekly

While it may seem strange to be so intentional about your physical contact, it is particularly important in the first few months after your loss because during this time, many couples experience conflict over intimacy. To some extent, this happens after any birth. However, the difficulties that grieving parents face go beyond the usual challenges that all new parents grapple with. For one thing, grieving parents are often ready to resume sexual intimacy at different times. Additionally, many partners are hesitant to seek intimacy because they are afraid of rejection and don't want to appear to be insensitive to their partner's ongoing grief. At times, one or both partners struggle with depression and find help through medications which can often have side effects that disrupt sexual arousal and interest.

It is important that partners attempt to understand the challenges that their loved one is facing when it comes to sexual intimacy. Parents who have not given birth are often very protective of partners that experienced pregnancy. They fear that they may physically harm their partner in some way and worry about what would happen to their partner if they were to become pregnant again. These worries may include practical and physical concerns as well as fears about their partner's emotional capacity to weather another pregnancy. Additionally, some parenting couples find that memories of their baby's traumatic birth inhibit their sexual drive.

Partners who have given birth, on the other hand, often struggle with low self-esteem related to their body image. This can be particularly intense because grieving parents may view their bodies as responsible for their baby's death. As one mother wrote, "I hated myself, I blamed myself, I couldn't even look at myself in a mirror. I was disgusted with my body, how I looked, how I felt - my daughter had died and I had been unable to protect her."

Other women find that sexual intimacy triggers flashbacks to their baby's traumatic deliveries. Additionally, some may have difficulty separating their sexuality from their baby. They report not wanting their partner to enter "the last place the baby was" because it somehow feels like a violation of sacred space, or they associate their uterus and vagina with death, making sexual intercourse repulsive to them. For example, one mother wrote, "I had an extremely traumatic and scary delivery when our daughter was stillborn. Afterwards, I couldn't associate 'down-there' with anything nice or positive."

If you find yourself facing any of these challenges, it is important that you talk openly with your partner about them. This will allow you to express your needs and reduces the chances that your partner will feel rejected. Lastly, it will give your partner the opportunity to help you overcome these hurdles together.

Finally, while issues related to sexual intimacy can be emotionally charged and difficult even in the best circumstances, remember that they are especially common after infant loss. You and your partner are not alone, and there is nothing "wrong" with either of you. Fortunately, these difficulties usually fade over time, especially with awareness and attention. If you find that your struggles are lingering, I encourage you to seek support from a therapist.

8. Get Help

Everything that I have written so far assumes a vital characteristic of your relationship: you are both truly committed to your relationship and to each other's well-being. Unfortunately, for some couples, this is not the case. Sometimes one or both parents struggle with addictions or mental illnesses that make it difficult or impossible to prioritize their partner's needs. At other times, infidelities or indifference prevent couples from truly coming together as a supportive team. In the worst situations, one or both partners is abusive, creating a dangerous, toxic environment.[23]

If one of these situations describes your relationship, I encourage you to seek professional guidance to determine how to move forward to a healthier place. Depending on your situation, therapists, counselors, sponsors, or hotline advocates can guide you to choose what steps your family should take to heal. Seeking help makes many people feel nervous, but you can harness your courage by remembering that getting the support you need is a vital step toward helping you parent your sunshine child.

CHAPTER TEN: SELF-CARE FOR MOTHERS

"When a parent dies, they are buried in the ground. When a child dies, they are buried in the parent's heart."
- A Proverb

What you are going through is so far beyond what anyone else can imagine - yet you are not alone in your ocean of sorrow and you can get through this! Surviving will take more strength, determination and perseverance than you ever knew you had. To overcome your grief and ensure that you are available to parent your sunshine child, you must care for yourself.

Grief is physically demanding. In fact, people who are bereaved have been found to have higher rates of illness, stomach problems, allergies, chronic diseases, cancer, and even premature death. Appendix I contains a checklist that you can use to track your self-care when your mind is preoccupied with grief. As you will see, the important things to attend to are also the basics: good rest, healthy food, and exercise. It is also critical that you carve out time to process your emotions.

Post-partum Recovery

Pregnancy is rough! For some people, it is more challenging than for others. While I am grateful that I was able to carry and grow my children within me, I hated being pregnant! Each of my three pregnancies was miserable, in part because of the complications I faced. However, even a by-the-book pregnancy that is free from complications takes a toll on the body.

For some bereaved parents, pregnancy is even more physically taxing than usual. Pregnancy complications like infections, problems with blood sugar, eclampsia, grueling inductions, and emergency c-sections all add to the list of things must ultimately heal. As a result, post-partum recovery after infant loss may require intense physical self-care.

If you recently delivered your baby, the hospital probably discharged you with instructions on wound care, what to expect, and warning signs that something is not right and needs medical attention. If any of these instructions are unclear, ask your care team to help you to understand. Your medical providers want you to be healthy and they are invested in making sure that you can take care of yourself once you leave the hospital. Consequently, your doctor and their staff should be your primary resources as you seek to heal your body. That being said, most of the information that hospitals send home is not specific to recovery after the loss of a baby. As a result, your care team's directions may not cover all of the topics that you might have questions about. This section will highlight some of these potential issues that can arise after a baby's death.

1. Bleeding

Vaginal bleeding, which is called lochia in this context, is expected after the birth of a baby. The amount varies depending on the type of birth you had. People tend to bleed less after a C-section than a vaginal delivery. Your hospital should give you guidance about what is a normal amount of blood to lose, how long you should expect to bleed, and how big any clots should be. If you find that you are bleeding more than the normal amount or that you are passing large clots of blood, do not hesitate to call your medical provider. You may be asked to return to the hospital, or you may be instructed to rest and monitor yourself at home.

You may find that you start bleeding more heavily if you are too active. As a result, if your bleeding increases you should put your feet up and give yourself some time to rest. In my case, after Noemi's funeral, I spent the rest of the day in bed because I was more active during her funeral and began to bleed more heavily during the reception.

Lochia after infant loss can be emotionally triggering because it is a vivid and constant reminder of your baby's death. If it is hard for you to see your blood, remind yourself that it will end. Then let yourself feel whatever surfaces for you. Handling these emotions is part of your healing process and accepting them now will help you to work through them so that they do not continue to haunt you over time.

2. Pain

Not surprisingly, you are likely to experience some level of pain during your physical recovery from pregnancy and delivery. Your arms and back might ache from pushing, your vaginal area may be tender and torn, you may have hemorrhoids and your incisions may throb. Talk with your doctor about what you can do to safely manage your pain. They will be able to come up with a plan that will work for you.

I was fortunate to have a team that was sensitive to my pain management needs after Noemi's death. The physician sat down with me and said, "You have enough emotional pain, you don't need to have any physical pain right now if you don't want to." I agreed and welcomed medications that eliminated most of my physical discomfort. Depending on your health history, this level of pain control may not be an option for you, but your care team should be able to provide you with some amount of relief from your physical pain, even after leaving the hospital.

Pain management is important because when your pain is well controlled, you are more likely to get up and move around. Being mobile helps you to heal more quickly and minimizes the amount of muscle you lose. Additionally, movement is a good way to avoid blood clots. In this sense, pain management is a critical part of your healthcare because it promotes healing and avoids unnecessary medical complications. From a psychological standpoint, it also lowers your level of stress and risk of postpartum depression. For these reasons, pain management is not just about comfort – it is about maximizing your ability to heal. Do not feel badly about asking for assistance in managing your pain.

Whiles controlling your pain is crucial, doctors are increasingly aware that some pain medications are highly addictive. Therefore, there is some incentive to minimize your use of these medications as much as possible. In fact, you might have concerns about addiction yourself. If this is the case, have an honest conversation with your provider so that you can develop a plan to manage your pain in a way that is acceptable to both of you. When it comes to handling your discomfort, only you can know what you need, so do not hesitate to advocate for yourself.

It should go without saying that it is important to take the correct dose of whatever your physician prescribes at the right time. However, this can be challenging in the days after your baby's death because you are likely fatigued, overwhelmed and possibly impacted by your medication. In my case, I struggled to remember which pills I had already taken after Noemi was born. Thankfully, my husband assumed the role of medication dispenser and gave me what I needed at the right time. When he went back to work, he made a list of medications and the times that I took each one so that I could check the doses off as the day progressed. I used an alarm to remind me to take the appropriate medications at the right time. Using my husband's simple method, I have included a sample medication chart in Appendix II to help you keep track of your medication doses.

Of course, medicine is not the only way you can alleviate pain. The following may also make you more comfortable:

- Ice packs for vaginal/breast/chest pain
- Heating pads for cramps, c-section incision, and sore muscles
- Sitz baths for vaginal pain and hemorrhoids

- Witch hazel wipes or pads for perineal tear or hemorrhoids
- Dermoplast numbing spray for perineal tears
- Donut pillows for soreness when sitting (a coiled maternity pillow serves the same purpose)
- Holding a pillow against your lower abdomen when riding in a car after a c-section
- Aromatherapy
- Massage
- Acupuncture
- Gentle movements like walking

3. Phantom cries and kicks

When a person loses a body part, their mind often has trouble making sense of this loss. As a result, their brain interprets signals from other parts of their body as coming from the limb that no longer exists. This makes the person "feel" pain in a limb that is no longer there. In psychology, we call these sensations "phantom limbs."[24] In a similar trick of the bereaved mind, many mothers feel "phantom kicks" and hear "phantom cries" after their baby's death. These illusions are a jarring reminder of what was once anticipated and lost.

The type of phantoms experienced after infant loss are unique. While phantom cries and kicks are most common in the days immediately following the baby's death, they can also happen later. While they can be unsettling, they are often a "normal" part of grief and do not indicate mental illness or psychosis. In fact, thinking that you hear or see a deceased loved one is a common grief experience after any kind of loss.

Psychology Nerd Moment: Phantoms in the Brain

Sandra Blakeslee and V.S. Ramachandran wrote a fascinating book called *Phantoms in the Brain* which explains the neuropsychology behind phantom limbs and other brain "hiccups." It is a great read!

My phantom experiences mostly happened at night as I was falling asleep and when I was transitioning from sleeping to waking. Since sleep had offered me an escape from my loss, the repetitive experience of phantom kicks made waking up painful and difficult. Often, I needed to take a few moments to transition from the peace of my dream to reality. I also needed to prepare myself for the return of my grief. Consequently, I learned to be gentle with myself and to experience sadness even at inconvenient times. This was an important part of working through my grief.

4. First Period After Your Baby's Delivery

At some point, you will start to menstruate again. The exact timing of this will vary depending on a variety of factors including how far along you were in your pregnancy and the amount of time you have lactated. In general, periods return within the first few months after a baby's death.

Your first period after your pregnancy may be more difficult than usual. You might find that you bleed more heavily and that you have more painful cramping. In addition, you may see more brown blood and blood clots. All of this is normal but if you are concerned for any reason, do not hesitate to talk with your physician.

In addition to the physical aspects of your first menstrual cycle, you will likely find that your emotions are more volatile than usual. In part, this is because your hormones are fluctuating drastically which is entirely normal during menstruation after a pregnancy. However, the return of your period can also force you to confront the reality of your baby's death with every cramp and changed pad. Your emotional reactions to your period might take you by surprise. This was the case for me. I was on vacation with my family when my period returned and I began to cry as soon as I realized. It made my sorrow about Noemi's death feel fresh and raw again.

Given the unpredictability of when your period will return, it is wise to be prepared. Doctors often want patients to only use pads during their first period post-pregnancy, so if you usually use tampons or menstrual cups, be sure to ask if those are safe to use. Make sure that you have the supplies you need on hand so that you are prepared whenever your period does come.

The return of your menstrual cycle is a sign that your body is healing and preparing itself for the possibility of another pregnancy. However, depending on the circumstances, your doctor may encourage you to wait for a certain amount of time before becoming pregnant again. Additionally, you may not be emotionally ready for another pregnancy. In these situations, it is important to have a plan to avoid conception, since it is possible to become pregnant before you are physically or emotionally prepared to do so.[25] If needed, your doctor can help you to develop a plan to manage your fertility in a way that honors medical history, personal preferences, and religious beliefs.

5. Weird Things

Many parents who lose an infant struggle with things that are less understood and sometimes have no logical cause. For example, for months after Noemi was born, I was convinced that I smelled horrible "down there." The smell was so potent to me that I was sure that it was offensive to those around me. However, when I reluctantly booked an appointment with my OB, he told me that I was physically okay and that I did not actually smell. Instead, he said that, in his experience, it is not uncommon for people to believe that they smell after childbirth. Since that time, I have encountered discussions of this phenomenon a few times, but it seems that it has never been researched and it is rarely discussed.

Similarly, bereaved parents often talk about having difficulty losing their pregnancy weight. Some people feel that they struggle because they subconsciously associate their extra pregnancy weight with their baby. The rationale is that the loss of the pregnancy weight will result in an added loss of connection with their baby.

I was surprised to discover that I had mixed feelings about finally getting back to my pre-pregnancy weight three years and three pregnancies later. I had been working hard for months to reach that goal and yet I hit a weight loss plateau right before losing those last extra pounds. In fact, it was not until I made the connection between my weight and my pregnancy with Noemi's that I was able to reach my goal. Apparently, it was important for me to acknowledge what losing those pounds meant to me – both the good and the bad. Once I did that, I was able to literally let the extra weight go.

I suspect that there are many other unusual ways that bereaved parents respond to their grief. Sadly, because our society does not talk about these things openly, these experiences remain unacknowledged, unidentified, and unresearched. In a way, it makes sense that infant death, which goes against the natural order of things, would cause "unnatural" responses in grieving parents. After all, is it possible to respond normally to an abnormal situation?

If you find yourself wrestling with something that you fear is "weird," do not struggle alone. Family, friends, support groups, medical professionals and therapists can all be sources of information and strength as you face even the strangest of issues. You may find that others do find your responses to your loss unusual. However, I have learned firsthand that even the most bizarre of these troubles eventually fade away and become no more than a memory. The chances are good that one day, you will think about whatever it is that is concerning you now and remark, "Oh yeah, I remember that!"

So, if something unusual is bothering you today, allow yourself to simply acknowledge its presence and the impact that it has on you. Then, remember that it will not last forever – nothing ever does. Often, this simple act of letting go will make even the most unpleasant situations easier to bear.

6. Hormones and Emotions

Make no mistake about it, the fact that you chose to focus on how to help your sunshine child by reading this book proves that you are a warrior. Rather than surrendering to overwhelming grief, you are fighting for you and your Sunshine! But even warriors cannot control the stealthy chemicals that flood in and out of their brains and wreak havoc with their emotions. When they become our enemy, hormones, particularly post-partum hormones, are formidable opponents.

Our bodies house various chemical pathways that intersect and function to sustain and animate our life. Hormones are chemicals that carry and influence messages across many of those networks. For example, hormones prompt our body systems to grow, change and act in certain ways. During pregnancy, delivery and lactation, the body harnesses these chemical messengers to ensure that a series of events happen at precisely the right time so that a baby can develop. When a pregnancy ends, there is a period adjustment while hormones settle out.

In addition to impacting our physical body, hormones also have a strong influence over our emotions. It is not surprising then that during the postpartum period, hormonal fluctuations can cause parents to feel like they are riding on an emotional roller coaster. Rapid and ongoing changes in estrogen, progesterone, thyroid, and stress hormone levels can leave even the strongest warrior parents reeling during the postpartum period. This can cause real problems for new parents.

In fact, between fifty and eighty percent of mothers experience transient "baby blues" in the first week postpartum. Additionally, up to twenty-three percent of them experience thyroid dysfunction in the weeks after their pregnancy. Sadly, up to one in four women will experience a major depressive episode following pregnancy, and hormones are largely responsible. Clearly, if your hormones are giving you trouble, you are not alone!

While hormones have a major impact on our moods and emotions, we must be careful not to let them distract or blind us to underlying problems in our lives. History is filled with cases of women whose concerns were brushed aside and dismissed as "just hormones" or an aspect of being "the weaker sex" (you don't need to look any further than the word "hysteria", the root of which – *hystericus* - means from the womb, which was historically used to explain away all kinds of female problems). Similarly, aggression in men is too often excused as the natural result of testosterone.

Unfortunately, hormones are often blamed as the source of emotional reactions to legitimate issues. The result is that the problems that trigger these reactions remain unaddressed. For example, far too many angry women have had their legitimate anger dismissed by some version of the question, "When is your period due, dear?" The tendency to blame any emotional response on hormonal imbalances is a dangerous one because it keeps us from addressing the real issues that are causing those emotions. It is important to recognize that powerful emotional reactions during the hormonally charged post-partum period are often triggered by real problems. One could say that the fact that we react at all indicates that there is an issue that needs to be addressed.

I think of it this way. When I am at my best, I have a certain threshold for ignoring things that are upsetting to me. Sometimes, my hormones lower this threshold and cause me to react more quickly and powerfully than I would at other times. This does not mean that what upsets me doesn't require my attention. In fact, the opposite is often true and too often I have been ignoring genuine problems to maintain the status quo. However, just because I can usually power through or ignore the problem does not mean that everything is okay. Part of caring for myself (so that I can care for my sunshine child) is addressing those stressors that become apparent when I am hormonally vulnerable. By responding in situationally appropriate ways, I ensure that these issues do not continue to cause problems for me and my family.

Other Babies

Mothers who have given birth to a baby who died often struggle when they encounter other infants and infant related events. Visiting playgrounds and attending baby showers can cause heartbreak. Meeting a friend's baby can provoke tears. An unexpected baptism at church can leave you feeling depleted and raw.

Experiencing distress when you encounter reminders of your loss is normal and there are few more potent reminders of your baby's death than the presence of other infants. Just because this is normal, however, does not mean it is easy to cope with. I have four suggestions for handling this kind of pain[26]:

1. Protect Your Heart

If something hurts too much, do not do it. It is okay to only bring your sunshine child to the playground when all the other kids and their baby siblings are napping. It is acceptable to send a note and gift rather than to attend a baby shower in person. It is appropriate to ask your ob-gyn to schedule your postpartum appointments at the start of the day before other patients arrive. It is alright to arrange visits with your close friends without their children. Be sensitive to what you are feeling and allow yourself to come up with solutions that will minimize your pain.

2. Give the Benefit of the Doubt

Grieving parents are easily wounded by those whose journey has not involved loss. For example, I have heard people say that an invitation to a baby shower feels like a slap in the face. At the same time, other people may feel excluded when their friends or family intentionally did not invite them to a shower to avoid hurting them. These reactions are both understandable. However, quick responses may result in damage to important relationships.

It can be helpful to detach from initial emotional responses and to try to think about the situation more pragmatically. In the example given above, once emotions are put aside, it is easy to see how a person who is a good friend may be in a bind when they are considering how to approach their grieving friend. They may not know what their friend needs and might make the wrong decisions about how to walk with their friend through grief.

Baby loss is such a painful experience that our emotional reactions are often unpredictable and not necessarily rational. Often, perceived insults are the result of our own grief tarnishing even our dearest relationships. Tragically, when we allow ourselves to nurture these grievances, we sever ourselves from people we care about at precisely the time when we need them most.

As difficult as it may be, I suggest that whenever you feel slighted, take a moment to breathe. Then broaden your perspective and consider if there might be a different, more benign motivation that could be behind the perceived hurt. Ask yourself if your friend's action could have been the result of a simple mistake or error in misjudgment? Consider that your interpretation might be wrong. Make a conscious choice to give the person who offended you the benefit of the doubt, particularly if they have shown themselves to be a good, caring friend to you in the past.[27] Podcaster Leah Darrow learned to approach the wounds that people unintentionally inflicted on her by saying, "I won't receive their words, but I will receive their intention. I will receive their intention of love and of support. Their intention of community and of kindness. I will receive that."

3. Ask To Hold the Other Baby If You Are Ready

Mothers who lose an infant frequently say that their arms literally ache to hold a baby. If you find yourself experiencing such longing, it may help to hold your friends' babies. In the weeks before and after Noemi was born, both my cousin and a good friend gave birth. Initially, I had mixed feelings about this. On the one hand, I was genuinely happy for these two women I cared about and their healthy little ones. On the other hand, their babies reminded me of the plans that we had made to have our children grow up together.

The first time I met their babies, neither of these women knew what to do. Despite their discomfort, they were wise and thoughtful, letting me take the lead while they cradled their little ones. Ultimately, when I asked to hold their babies, they seemed relieved and were eager for me to do so. It gave them a chance to offer something that could help me in a tangible way. It also created a space for us to talk about how uncomfortable they felt having their baby around me when I had lost mine. As a result, we were able to share our grief. At the same time, holding each of these precious children was healing for me, soothing my aching, empty arms. In fact, I still vividly remember the happiness and wonder I felt when one of the babies gave me his first smile...an amazing gift!

4. Anticipate Anxiety When Friends Are Pregnant

Do not be surprised if you are anxious when your friends are pregnant or in labor, even after your own grief has become less intense. You will never again entertain the blissful delusion that a woman who gets past the first trimester is safe. Similarly, you now know that not every woman who enters the hospital in labor will leave with a healthy baby a few days later. In fact, whenever you hear that someone is pregnant, you will probably hear a little voice in your head saying, "This might not end well!" If you care about the person, this can make you anxious. I experienced this recently when one of my best friends texted me to tell me she was in labor. I was uneasy until I got the text saying that her baby was safely delivered and healthy.

In addition to my concern for her and her baby's arrival, I was also surprised to find that I felt on the verge of crying for several days after her baby's birth. I began to have vivid nightmares about Noemi's death. These unanticipated reactions surprised me. They also helped me to realize that my mind still perceives birth as something that is traumatic. This recognition, coupled with accepting my feelings and seeking support, allowed me to work through this reactivated grief with minimal disruptions to the life that I have worked to build since Noemi's death.

Raising Sunshine

CHAPTER ELEVEN: LACTATION

"It's fear of the milk, because milk is a trigger, a threat, an emotionally-charged, natural, physical response, but just a nasty killer of a reminder of the loss..."
- Lactation Consultant who participated in a study by Catherine Waldby, et al.

Lactation is a physical part of grieving an infant death and its significance is easily overlooked. It is an unavoidable issue that most grieving families must deal with and it can cause significant distress.

When a baby dies after about the sixteenth week of pregnancy, most mothers will begin to produce milk after delivery. Additionally, a baby who dies after a full-term pregnancy often leaves behind a mother who has worked hard to establish their milk supply. This leaves grieving families in the uncomfortable position of having to figure out what to do with milk that is no longer needed. While I was unaware of this issue prior to Noemi's death, I have since learned that there are a few different approaches that parents can take in response to this dilemma.

As you consider which method will work best for you and your family, know that every mother reacts to lactation differently. For some parents, like Elizabeth Peszat, terminating lactation can feel like a continuation of their loss. She wrote, "I had already said goodbye, but this was another ending." As a result, it is important that you pay attention to your own needs and do not feel pressured into a particular choice. There are very few, if any "should" in this journey of healing after infant loss. How you decide to handle your lactation is not one of them. It is your choice and yours alone.

Milk Suppression

Lactation after the death of an infant is often a painful reminder of excruciating loss. When combined with the hormones that the lactation process releases, milk production can be unbearable. For this reason, the milk of bereaved mothers has been called "white tears." Given the emotional toll that lactation after infant loss can take, many parents choose to suppress milk production soon after their baby's death.

Still, some do not find lactation to be as emotionally charged, but they decide to suppress their milk supply for other valid reasons which may include health concerns, the impact on careers, logistical decisions, disliking lactation, body image and gender dysphoria, and other quality of life issues. For example, when I nursed my sunshine child, I suffered from recurrent mastitis which resulted in surgery. While I was willing to risk repeating that experience if Noemi could benefit from my milk supply, I wanted to avoid this after her death.

Historically, if a mother needed to suppress lactation, they were given medications that dried up their supply. However, these drugs are now known to carry health risks[28] and many doctors today will no longer prescribe them. Instead, mothers must suppress their lactation naturally, a process that takes several weeks and some planning to avoid problems.[29] While it can be difficult to navigate, there are things that you can do to ease the process as detailed in the table that follows.

Choosing to Continue Lactating

While many parents do opt to suppress milk production after infant loss, others choose to continue lactating. In these cases, lactation provides comfort, a sense of physical closeness to the baby, confirmation, and reassurance that the baby existed. Sometimes it provides mothers with an opportunity to embrace their identity as a parent. The process also allows time and space to grieve the parenting experiences that will not be. Other parents choose to lactate because of its health benefits, such as reduced rates of breast cancer, natural family planning, lower likelihood of postpartum depression, and enhanced loss of pregnancy weight. There are also families who choose to donate their milk to a baby whose own mother cannot feed them.

The basic approach to building or sustaining your milk supply is similar for all mothers and it is outlined in the following table. If you find yourself struggling in any way, certified lactation consultants can be a wonderful resource.

What To Do with the Milk You Pump or Express

While many parents discard their milk after their baby dies, there are several ways to use it. These include:

- ✓ Freeze it while you decide what to do
- ✓ Freeze it indefinitely as a tangible reminder of your baby
- ✓ Donate it to babies whose parents cannot breast/chestfeed
- ✓ Donate it to science and research
- ✓ Have it made into a memento (there are companies that take breastmilk and form it into things like jewelry)

As noted, parents who do not discard their milk may choose to donate it. You can do this formally through a milk bank or more casually through a milk share.[30]

If you decide to donate to a milk bank, you need to follow their protocols. Milk banks have intensive safety measures in place to protect the babies who receive donations, and these necessarily restrict the types of donations that can be accepted. For example, parents who take medications while they are lactating may be ineligible to donate milk. While it can be frustrating to jump through so many hoops, know that such increased scrutiny and caution protects the babies that you want to help. This is especially important because many vulnerable NICU babies depend on milk from milk banks as their only source of breast milk. If your milk qualifies for donation, you may be charged a fee or asked to donate a minimum amount. Many milk banks will waive these requirements for bereaved parents when asked.

If you want to donate your milk but choose not to go through a milk bank, there are less formal milk share options available. Online groups may organize sharing directly between the donating and receiving parents. These tend to be more relaxed in terms of requirements and have minimal, if any, health restrictions. Still, informal milk shares have some potential drawbacks due to the direct interactions that occur between donors and recipients. For many parents, navigating these relationships is not difficult and their milk-sharing arrangements are healing. However, for some parents, the relationship can be painful or even contentious, particularly when the recipient family expects things that the donor cannot give. Consequently, it is important to establish boundaries and expectations right from the beginning of your milk sharing relationship.

Tips for Suppressing or Sustaining Lactation				
What Are You Trying to Accomplish?	Suppress Unestablished Supply	Suppress Established Supply	Build a Supply to Continue Lactating	Maintain an Established Supply
Remove Enough Milk to Relieve Pressure[31]	✓	✓		
Soothe Breasts with Cold Packs and Cabbage Leaves	✓	✓		
Avoid Heat	✓	✓		
Gradually Reduce the Amount of Milk You Express[32]	✓	✓		

Use Pain Medications as Needed	✓	✓		
Use a Hospital Grade Pump[33]		✓	✓	✓
Drink Sage and Peppermint Tea	✓	✓		
Wear a Comfortable Bra All Day and Night[34]	✓	✓	✓	✓
Take Prescribed Supplements and Vitamins	✓	✓	✓	✓
Use Nursing Pads for Leaks	✓	✓	✓	✓
Drink Lots of Liquids	✓	✓	✓	✓
Avoid Caffeine and Alcohol	✓	✓	✓	✓
Completely Drain Breasts and Continue Pumping			✓	✓
Pump Every Few Hours			✓	✓
Pump in a Comfortable, Relaxed Position			✓	✓

Store Milk Properly			✓	✓
Don't Worry if Your Body Stops Producing Milk on its Own			✓	✓
Begin Pumping Sessions with Several Minutes on the Stimulation Setting			✓	
Once Milk Stops Flowing, Continue Pumping on the Stimulation Setting for Several Minutes			✓	
Don't Worry If You Don't Produce Much Milk at First			✓	
Continue Pumping on the Same Schedule You Have Been Using to Pump or Nurse				✓

Lactation Pitfalls

Sometimes, no matter how carefully you manage your milk production, you end up with one of the three most dreaded lactation pitfalls: engorgement, plugged ducts or mastitis. While painful and frustrating, these complications do not mean you have failed in your efforts to produce or suppress your milk supply. Instead, they are an indication that you need to give yourself extra care and may have to approach your lactation goals more gradually. It is important that you address these health issues promptly because, if they are ignored, they can cause more challenging problems. The following table can help you to troubleshoot these three hazards and figure out how to overcome them.

Lactation Pitfalls		
Problem	**Symptoms**	**Suggestions**
Engorgement	Breasts are: • Swollen • Hard • Painful	• Fully express your milk so that you completely empty your breasts (if you are trying to suppress your milk production, only do this once and then empty just enough to remain comfortable and avoid engorgement) [35] • Apply cool packs or frozen to your breasts for comfort
Plugged Duct	Hard, painful spot on the breast	• Massage the painful area of the breast in toward your nipple until the duct releases[36] • If massaging alone doesn't work, run warm water over your breast while you

		massage
		• Watch the tender spot to make sure that the milk continues to flow and it does not become blocked again
		• Drink plenty of fluids
		• If you experience plugged ducts repeatedly, talk to a doctor or lactation consultant about using lecithin supplements to thin your milk
Mastitis	Breast/chest is: • Red • Painful • Hot Often, there is a painful lump that you cannot work out and you may have: • Fever • Flu-like symptoms • Body Aches • Chills • Fatigue	• Contact your doctor right away[37] • Completely drain your breast at regular intervals until the mastitis has resolved[38]

CHAPTER TWELVE: FOR FATHERS AND OTHER PARTNERS

"Grief is the price we pay for love."
- Queen Elizabeth II

As is obvious by now, the emotional responses of parents who lose a child are highly variable. Even within a single individual, reactions can fluctuate from profound sorrow to numbness. Sometimes, the same parent feels multiple emotions at once. Know that you have every right to feel whatever and however about your baby's death.

Some parents feel intense emotions immediately after their baby dies, making it impossible to carry on with the business of living. They are devastated by their child's death and this may take them by surprise. These parents rage, weep, or avoid reminders of their loss. Some are reserved about their pain, while others talk about it openly. Still others find ways to articulate their experience creatively. For example, the music artist Prince wrote the song "Comeback" after his son died shortly after birth.

Other parents may feel somewhat detached from their loss, or even from their lives. This may be particularly true of fathers and non-gestational mothers who did not have a chance to bond with the baby through the physical experience of pregnancy. While these parents are sad, the pain may feel blunted or distant and less overwhelming to them. However, even these mothers and fathers will likely experience the loss of years' worth of hopes and dreams that they had for their baby.

I encourage you to accept wherever you find yourself on the spectrum of grief. Your emotions are all valid responses to your baby's death. The feelings themselves are neutral – neither right nor wrong. It is what you do with your emotions that matters and will ultimately make a difference for you and your sunshine child. The most important thing is to acknowledge your feelings, accept them, and do whatever is necessary to care for yourself as you experience them.

Sidelined

You have probably already noticed that a parent who has not given birth tends to be forgotten in the wake of infant loss. Even before leaving the hospital, almost all of the attention is directed toward the birth parent, and this remains true once you return home. As Kelly Farley, author of *Grieving Dads: To the Brink and Back*, said, "People would always ask me how my wife was doing and they never asked how I was doing." You may have even participated in sidelining yourself by focusing so much on caring for your grieving family that your own sense of loss gets pushed aside. In your mind, you may view your feelings as secondary or less important than those of the mother.

Because your experience of loss is so often forgotten, it is easy to feel isolated. For some parents, this complicates their pain. They may question if it is even normal for them to respond to their own sense of loss when no one seems to expect them to.

If this rings true for you, trust that you are not alone and there are things you can do to express your own grief and feel heard. For example, try framing your answers to questions in a way that includes you. If your friend says, "How is your wife doing?" you can reply, "Well, it is obviously really tough and *we* are having a hard time with it." Another option is to seek out time with someone you can really talk to, whether that is your partner or a good friend. Be open and honest with them so that they can understand what you are experiencing. Often, the simple knowledge that someone cares can lessen the sting of otherwise being overlooked.

On the other hand, some parents, like my husband, are most comfortable when they remain in the periphery while their partner is the center of attention. They recognize their partner's need for support and are glad they are receiving what they need. Due to their more introverted and private personalities, they are reluctant to share their own emotions and are most comfortable when they can grieve more privately.

Whether you long for someone to ask you about how you are doing, or you are relieved that the attention is off of you, the important thing is for you to be able to recognize your own needs and figure out how to meet them. It is impossible to control what other people do and do not do. However, you can control how you respond to them, as well as how much you prioritize your own self-care. If you are feeling unsupported by your community, take some time to figure out what it would take to make you feel more supported, and then work to make that happen.

Talk with Your Partner

Many parents are reluctant to rely on their partners for support because they are afraid that they will be a burden. They feel that, rather than needing support themselves, they should be their family's caregiver and comforter. While there are times and situations when a partner is truly incapable of being supportive, most couples that I have encountered agree that sharing their grief is a source of comfort for both of them. For example, one father wrote that when he tried to protect his wife by not talking about his own grief, his efforts actually caused her more heartache because she felt that he had withdrawn from her when she needed his companionship the most.

In my own marriage, it took time for my husband to articulate his thoughts and feelings about our daughter's death. The first time he did, I felt relief for many reasons:

1. It helped me to understand his perspective on the events that led to and followed our daughter's death.

2. I could make sense of and anticipate his behavior more effectively.

3. I felt more comfortable and less guilty about sharing my own sorrow.

4. Our shared emotions helped me to feel understood.

5. I had been worried about him, and this stress was relieved when he was able to express his emotions with me.

6. I was grateful for the opportunity to support him, rather than always being the one needing care and support.

Often, fathers forget that their partners want to be their helpmates. Memories of birth trauma and the fear of losing their partner during pregnancy often make them particularly protective of their loved one. They lose sight of the fact that their partner does not want to be the only one who is protected and cared for.

I firmly believe that very few people who love one another want to be like Sleeping Beauty: laying around with the sole purpose of looking lovely while their mate battles dragons for them. Instead, most of us hope to be more like Frodo and Sam Gamgee: caring for one another and bearing each other's burdens to make the bad more tolerable. This is what it means to be partners in every sense of the word.

If you are hesitant to add to your partner's sorrows by sharing your own, consider the probability that your partner wants to fight this battle beside you. If you do not share your anguish and despair with them, you will be depriving them of the chance to both love and be loved in a powerful way. If you can be vulnerable with your partner, you have the chance to heal and support one another through what is likely to be the darkest time of your life. The choice is yours.

CHAPTER THIRTEEN: SPECIAL CONSIDERATIONS

"We have learned that when people ask how any of us are doing, and when they really listen to the answer with an open heart and mind, the load of grief often becomes lighter – for all of us. In being invited to share our pain, together we take the first steps towards healing."
- Meghan, Duchess of Sussex

So far, we have discussed issues that are applicable to most grieving families. However, certain groups of families face issues that are unique to them. While I cannot address every possible situation a family may encounter, my hope is that even those who find themselves in situations that I do not mention will recognize and find solace in the universal threads that bind us together in sorrow over the loss of our children. As Dr. Christa Craven, a grieving LGBTQ+ mother wrote, infant loss is "a human experience of love and hope and heartbreak and grief." It is a sorrow all bereaved parents know. I hope that this unified human experience will ease any feelings of isolation that you may encounter and help you to feel connected to a larger community of individuals who seek to parent well through their sorrow.

Parents Who Identify with a Minority Ethnic or Racial Group

The loss of an infant adds to the already heavy burden of marginalization that many families face. This is often the case for families who identify with a minority ethnic or racial group. In such families, the devastation of losing their child may be complicated by ongoing prejudice, discrimination and resulting trauma. Unfortunately, these same families often experience infant and maternal death more frequently than other families who are not living the realities of systemic racism.

Consider:

✓ Black women are three to four times more likely to die from complications during childbirth than are non-Hispanic, white women.

✓ Puerto Rican mothers are two times more likely to die in childbirth than non-Hispanic white mothers.

✓ When other risk factors (such as economic status) are removed, Thai infants are ninety percent more likely to die than their non-Hispanic White peers.

✓ American Indian/Alaskan Native and non-Hispanic Black babies are more likely to die from SIDS (Sudden Infant Death Syndrome).

✓ Black babies who are born to a college educated mother are five times more likely to die than babies born to white women with high school education, suggesting that socioeconomic factors are not the sole cause of high black infant mortality.

✓ When Black infants receive care from black doctors, they are significantly less likely to die, indicating that racial bias (whether implicit or explicit) impacts whether a child lives or dies.

While differences in infant mortality between various groups of people have traditionally been attributed to socioeconomic factors, there is increasing evidence that systematic health care disparities (including access to quality care) play a large role. As the March of Dimes notes, "Pregnancy and infant loss also happens more often among those groups who experience health disparities." There are multiple contributors to healthcare inequality, ranging from blatant acts of racism and other forms of prejudice by medical professionals, to a lack of diversity in medical research subjects. The latter can inadvertently result in the development of tools and norms that do not work as well for minority populations. For example, something as simple as an oxygen saturation monitor can be impacted by skin tone and something as complex as an IQ score can be impacted using ethnic names in the test.

Healthcare disparities create an environment in which infants from minority groups are at risk. It is therefore understandable that when one of these at-risk babies dies, their families experience a kind of anger and trauma that grieving white families do not face. If you find yourself wrestling with these emotions, I encourage you to seek support from knowledgeable faith leaders and mental healthcare providers. These professionals will be best equipped to help you as you work to heal from the death of your baby.

Unfortunately, it is common for many cultural and religious groups to look down on mental health care. This is often rooted in past experiences with mental health professionals who are, at best, culturally and religiously insensitive.[39] However, many cultures also share a belief that suffering people should be able to power through their difficulties to avoid looking weak or bringing shame to the family. While I do not mean to disregard these cultural norms, it is my hope that you will investigate the various ways that you can be supported during this time. Getting help can be incredibly valuable for your own healing and that of your sunshine child and our society is opening to the idea that it takes strength, courage, and honor to seek needed help.

Finally, one other factor that sometimes surfaces is that grieving rituals are often unique to specific minority communities. In some cultures, for example, an important way to mark a loved one's death is to make a commitment or promise to them. In others, it is necessary to carry out a burial in a particular way or amount of time. Sometimes, these traditions conflict with things like hospital policies. For instance, families may encounter difficulty getting their baby's body released to a trusted authority for proper burial. If you find yourself facing such problems, I encourage you to work with someone who can effectively advocate for you. This may mean asking for help from a community or faith leader. Hospital social workers and funeral home directors can also be very helpful in navigating these sorts of conflicts.[40]

LGBTQ+ Parents

The almost universal feelings of isolation that grieving parents experience seems to be more intensely felt by LGBTQ+ parents. Their loss is often minimized by the general community, particularly when the couple has not pursued parenthood in conventional ways. Additionally, most available literature and depictions of infant loss assume that grieving families are headed by a man and a woman, which can make the experiences of LGBTQ+ families facing infant loss feel unseen.

The profound loneliness that such assumptions cause is most challenging for non-gestational LGBTQ+ parents. Even before they leave the hospital, many of these parents report that prejudice and implicit bias compounded their grief. Often, these parents report being mistaken for a family friend or more distant relative, and such errors meant that staff excluded them from important conversations and decisions about care for their baby and, potentially, their partner. Additionally, fewer people expressed sympathy and support for them, which is a trend that continued after discharge from the hospital. Parents' feelings about these experiences often overlapped with their grief at the loss of their child. As one grieving LGBTQ+ mother wrote, "Our tears are not always only for ourselves, but for the cumulative losses that we and others have faced."

Many LGBTQ+ parents also faced legal hurdles which undermined their role as parent. One grieving parent explained that their family faced excessive medical bills when their insurance refused to recognize them as the parent of their child and would not insure the baby. Other families have found that the medical care they receive is negatively impacted by their status as LGBTQ+ parents. A disturbing number of patients have stories of being turned away when they sought treatment, having to travel great distances to find providers who are knowledgeable about the unique issues that face the LGBTQ+ community. Many families ultimately relocated to different areas to find these medical resources, but not all are financially able to make such a move.

Even without the impact of inhumane laws, biased medical treatment, and prejudice, many LGBTQ+ parents face financial difficulties while they grieve. Often, these parents have spent large amounts of money trying to have a baby and this can leave them in a financially precarious position that complicates their ability to grieve their infant's death.

The investment and effort that have been devoted to having a baby can also leave parents feeling like they have let the LGBTQ+ community down. These parents report that they wanted to prove their family was legitimate and that they could become the parents of a healthy baby just like any other family. When their baby died, they felt that they confirmed some people's belief that their family is not worthy of children. These feelings, although understandable, are particularly tragic since many families ultimately find that the death of their baby serves to connect them to a broader community of bereaved parents. Straight parents can identify with the grief that these LGBTQ+ parents face, establishing a path toward empathy and connection that did not exist prior to their infants' deaths.

If you and your partner are facing any of these difficulties, it is important that you allow yourself to feel whatever emotions they bring up. In addition, it is critical that you protect your heart as you grieve. This may mean that you must work to build a network of unprejudiced support and professional caregivers.

Some LGBTQ+ parents experience gender dysphoria during pregnancy and after childbirth. Generally, this occurs in parents who have wrestled with this in the past. For these parents, the entire process of pregnancy is triggering because so much of it is generally associated with female reproduction. Consequently, the systems and language that has evolved around pregnancy is highly gendered.

Another unique issue facing LGBTQ+ parents is that the growth or regrowth of chest tissue that occurs during and after pregnancy can be upsetting. In fact, lactation has been reported to increase symptoms of gender dysphoria. Handling chest related gender dysphoria is difficult for these parents because they cannot use chest binding until lactation has stopped naturally. Additionally, parents who do not identify with the gender to which they were assigned at birth often find that healthcare professionals and community members use the wrong pronouns when talking with them. This can contribute to heightened gender dysphoria, leading to an increased risk of mental health problems such as severe depression and anxiety. It can also alienate parents from the very people who are supposed to be providing guidance, care, and support.

If you find yourself struggling with any of these issues, I encourage you to seek social and professional support. To heal and parent your sunshine child, you need to make sure that both your physical and mental needs are being met by sensitive individuals who are knowledgeable about the specific issues facing LGBTQ+ parents and who can provide a safe place for you and your partner to process your emotions. While it may take some time to find the people who can best support you, it goes without saying that the effort will be worthwhile.

The following websites are a good place to start your search: Pregnancy & Infant Loss Support Centre (www.pilsc.org) and MISS Foundation (www.missfoundation.org). These websites welcome LGBTQ+ parents while offering resources and support groups. If you are not able to find what you need on these sites, consider reaching out to a larger hospital system that has a program designed specifically for LGBTQ+ patients. Cleveland Clinic, for example, has a Center for Lesbian, Gay, Bisexual, and Transgender (LGBTQ+) Care which specializes in addressing needs that are unique to LGBTQ+ individuals.[41] While these programs usually focus on primary care, they will likely be able to direct you with resources and knowledgeable providers within your local community.

It can be discouraging and overwhelming to find care but remind yourself that doing so is an investment in your sunshine child. By prioritizing your needs, you are increasing the odds that you will be able to successfully guide your child on their own journey through loss.

Blended Families

As cliché as it sounds, one of the first things that I learned working with families is that no two are alike. The parental relationships that adults forge with their children have life-long impacts that are powerful and unique. While no two blended families are the same, they often have similarities. For example, stepmother and author Laura Petherbridge pointed out that all blended families have one thing in common: loss. According to Petherbridge, "All stepfamilies are birthed out of loss... a death, a divorce, or the breakup of a relationship had to have occurred to create a stepfamily ...You have a lot of emotion that goes into a second relationship, or a remarriage, that you didn't have in a first time relationship. That is why it's complicated."

The common thread of loss means that these families must deal with certain issues that other families will never encounter. For example, in blended families, the traumas of past losses are often reawakened and inflamed by infant death. This is particularly true in families that formed after parental death. If you find that your baby's death triggers painful emotions from your past, it can feel especially dark and overwhelming. Acknowledge these emotions and allow yourself the space and time to wrestle with them.

While it can be frustrating to revisit grief that you thought was resolved, know that you are not starting at the beginning. Instead, you will

likely realize that your past grief has given you tools that will help you to manage your current sorrow. Despite experiencing profound disappointment and sadness in the past, you survived and you now have the hard earned survival skills needed to overcome grief at your disposal. You can use your knowledge to help you heal and to strengthen your sunshine child, too.

Know also that grief is not linear. The author of the Chronicles of Narnia, C.S. Lewis, described his grief over his wife's death thus, "For in grief, nothing 'stays put.' One keeps on emerging from a phase, but it always recurs. Round and round. Everything repeats." Like Lewis, many psychologists who study grief recognize its cyclical nature. You may circle back to old themes, but you will never encounter those themes in the same way. You have been changed by your earlier losses, and you will be changed by this one, but you will never be forced to start at the beginning again.

Another challenge that blended families encounter is a rising sense of resentment. Stepparents may wonder why their stepchild is able to live a normal life but their own child died. Such feelings of resentment are often unacknowledged because they make stepparents feel guilty, however, it is important to remember that they are normal responses to your grief. While your emotions are understandable, your responses to these feelings might make it difficult for you to maintain the family relationships that you cherish. Consequently, it is important that you figure out how to manage them and acknowledging that they exist is essential to beginning this process. Recognize and accept your feelings of resentment, but do not dwell on them. Rather, become more aware of when you are feeling resentful, what triggers these feelings, and how they impact your behavior so that you can control your responses to them. Remember, your goal is to love and protect your sunshine child even as you grieve. To achieve this goal, you may sometimes have to act in ways that contradict your emotions, including your resentment. Sometimes this is what love requires.

When I was a young child, I often wondered how my parents could keep loving me even after I had been very naughty (probably because I certainly did not feel love for them when they were the recipients of my wrath). My father told me, "Love isn't a feeling, it is an action. We love you, even when we do not feel it, because we have promised never to stop loving you." I share this story to illustrate that it is certainly possible to choose to love your stepchild, even if you are feeling resentment and anger at the injustice of the loss of your precious infant. In fact, it is often acts of love that are performed in the face of contradictory emotions that reveal the true strength of our love.

In families where one parent loses a stepchild, it is common for that parent to feel particularly isolated. While stepparents may experience the same grief reactions that biological parents do, their grief may be unacknowledged. Their hopes and dreams for their stepchild are forgotten while everyone's attention is focused on the biological parent. Grieving stepparents can feel left out of conversations, decision making, and even gestures of sympathy. Too often, their pain is minimized and ignored. However, stepparents have every reason to grieve for the child they lost. The Compassionate Friends information packet for grieving stepparents describes it thus: "Even though we do not have a biological or perhaps legal connection, the death of a child within our family circle is still going to be a terrible event." In some cases, it can be as profound a loss as losing a child who was biologically yours.

Sadly, grieving stepparents frequently feel isolated from their partners. They may or may not experience the extent of grief that their partner bears, but they certainly feel pain as they witness their loved one suffering. They may also feel confused about the ways in which their partner is responding to grief and resentful of their partner's focus on the loss. Additionally, while most stepparents want to help their grieving partners and step-sunshine children, they may not know how to do this and this can cause them to feel guilty or inadequate. Such responses are normal.

Regardless of how you respond to your own loss, you play a vital role in helping your loved ones grieve. Your respect for their wishes, willingness to be available to them, and reassuring presence are all extremely valuable to them. In fact, it is possible that you will draw closer to them during this time as you assume new, supportive roles within your family. Many parents find that their sunshine children and step-sunshine children are even more precious to them after the loss of an infant.

Tips for Co-parenting Well	
Respect Boundaries	• Establish clear expectations about your roles and interactions with one another • Be open to the possibility that some of these expectations may change after the death of an infant • Respect one another's boundaries
Focus on Your Child	• Keep your communication focused on important information about your sunshine child • Plan how to address the baby's death, keeping your Sunshine's needs in mind
Encourage Your Child to Love Your Co-Parent	• Be careful about how you talk about your co-parent in front of your sunshine child • Ensure that your Sunshine has time to bond with their other parent • Try to talk about your co-parent in a way that paints them in the best (but realistic) light possible • Think about your co-parent as an essential part of your sunshine child's support network
Communicate Well, Listen Better	• Think through what you want to say before you say it • Frame your concerns as issues that you need to address together instead of as an attack (for example, "When you talk about the fun your

	family is having, it makes me feel very sad because I remember what I won't be able to do with my own baby") • Focus on "I" statements (I feel, I think, I need, etc.) rather than "you" statements (you did, you made, you always, etc.) • Pay close attention to your body language • Clarify your understanding by saying something like, "I want to make sure I am understanding you correctly. I am hearing you say that you feel _____ because of _____. Is that that right?"
Be Selective	• Think of your relationship as a transaction: the more positive interactions you have, the better your relationship is and the more negative interactions you have, the more difficult your relationship becomes. Before you bring an issue up, decide whether it is important enough to potentially add to your pile of negative interactions. • Figure out what you must address and let go of what you can
Give the Benefit of the Doubt	• Assume that your co-parent will do their best to parent well • Remember that you are both under stress and are unsure of how to navigate your co-parenting and parenting relationship in this new situation so be patient with one another • Allow your co-parent to make mistakes without assuming that these are the result of character flaws

| Let Go | • Even if you do everything right (which you will not) you can only do so much to make your co-parenting relationship work. When you do your best and your co-parent is not able to meet you where you are, remember: |
| | • Your sunshine child is resilient and your desire to do what is best for your sunshine child is an incredible gift and help to them |

One final issue that can surface in blended families is related to co-parenting. Studies have shown that how families function after a divorce has a greater impact on children than the experience of divorce itself. In fact, multiple studies have found that children with divorced parents fare better when their parents co-parent well. So, a key way to help your child through their grief is to commit to making your relationship with your co-parents as effective as possible.[42] This can be done by doing what you can to keep your interactions cooperative, exchanging important information about one another, and treating your co-parent with respect. This is especially important when you must interact with your co-parent around your sunshine child. As much as possible, you and your co-parent should try to agree on parenting decisions. Of course, disagreements are inevitable and, when they happen, you should handle these conflicts in respectful, effective ways that prioritize what is best for your sunshine child. Additionally, strive to maintain healthy, flexible boundaries and expectations for one another.

So how do you do this? Simply by establishing that your goal is to do what is best for your sunshine child. You may not have as much control over your co-parenting relationship as you would like, but you can do your best to make it work as well as possible. In doing so, you provide your sunshine child with critical support.

Single Parents

All grieving parents feel isolated at some point, but these feelings can be particularly intense for parents who are flying solo.[43] Depending on why you are a single parent, you may have felt abandoned or even guilty before your baby died. These feelings may worsen and intensify after a baby dies.

In addition to feeling alone, you may be overwhelmed by all you have to do alone. When a baby dies, the demands of life do not cease even though you have less strength to meet them. To be able to keep going, you need to take the seemingly impossible step of meeting your own needs.

The key to taking care of yourself is ensuring that you have practical support lined up to help you through this time. Accept any offers of assistance. Ask friends and family for help and be specific about what you need.[44] In short, your goal is to become an expert delegator. To do this, you can consider asking trusted adults to assist with:

- ✓ Childcare
- ✓ Driving
- ✓ Funeral arrangements
- ✓ Handling the baby's possessions
- ✓ Groceries
- ✓ Cooking
- ✓ Cleaning
- ✓ Helping you find time to grieve on your own
- ✓ Preserving items that you want to keep as reminders of your baby
- ✓ Sharing news of your baby's death with your community
- ✓ Communicating with your sunshine child's school

Many solo parents have already developed a strong network of support. Others, however, may need to move outside of their comfort zones to find the help they need. Sometimes it is necessary to repair relationships that were previously damaged or broken. If someone offers to help, be courageous enough to accept, even if your relationship with this person has been difficult in the past.[45] If you need more support than your family and friends can provide, there may be organizations that can assist you. Your local library, church or other place of worship, physician's office, or local grief center can help you find the support you need. When Noemi died, we were impressed by the many ways that a local organization called the Children's Center provided for local, bereaved families. Since that time, we have learned about other such organizations that have touched the lives of grieving families across the country.

While getting everything done can be a challenge, solo parents often have an unrecognized advantage as they deal with the loss of their infant. Many of these parents have faced challenges in the past and have had to develop strategies to cope with them. Use that wisdom to meet the challenges that you are now facing.

What was most helpful to you when you faced unexpected difficulties in the past? Incorporate these strategies into your daily life and remember that, while parenting solo might feel overwhelming right now, you have the strength and creativity to get through this current struggle, too. When you do, your sunshine child will have learned important lessons from you about resourcefulness, acceptance, perseverance, and courage.

Kinship Caregivers and Foster Parents

While we don't often think of kinship caregivers and foster parents as grieving parents, in some cases, that is exactly what they are. Children in care are more likely to die than children who do not enter the foster care system and, tragically, sometimes decisions to reunify infants with their families result in their death. Since the role of a kinship or foster parent is to stand in for a child's birth parents, the ones who do their job well develop deep emotional bonds with the children in their care. These bonds carry over to their children as well, who often welcome foster and kinship children as siblings. As a result, kinship caregivers and foster families can experience the same emotions that other grieving families do. Not surprisingly, their grief is complicated in several ways.

Foster and kinship families who experience the death of a child in their care often experience a heightened sense of guilt since many families who care for a child who is not their own feel a strong obligation to the child's parents. They may feel that they failed in their role as the child's caregivers and that they failed to meet the parents' expectation that their child was being safely cared for.

If you find yourself struggling with such guilt, I recommend you use the strategies discussed in Chapter Fifteen to help you deal with this emotion. Additionally, Sunshine children who live in foster and kinship homes may worry that feelings of resentment or frustration towards their foster sibling contributed to their death. This may be particularly powerful for the biological children in these families because their acceptance of their parents' role as caregivers is often complicated. In these situations, it is important to reassure children that the baby's death was not their fault.

Kinship caregivers and foster parents whose foster child dies after being reunified with their birth family often experience intense anger and feelings of betrayal by the child welfare system. Many had significant concerns about their child's reunification, and they may feel that these concerns were ignored. Indeed, in a very real way, the system did fail both the foster or kinship parents and the baby.

It can be very difficult to know how to help a sunshine child to understand an infant's death after reunification. The circumstances surrounding the baby's death are likely horrific and impossible for adults to come to terms with, so sharing such news with Sunshine children seems unimaginable. Additionally, the impact of this death is sometimes complicated by the fact that the siblings were separated at reunification and so they already grieved the loss of their sibling at that time. For very young children, it may be best to wait until the child is older to share what happened. Older children or children who continued to have contact with their foster sibling after reunification will need to be told what happened in age-appropriate ways. Supporting them through this process may be particularly frightening and difficult. Do not hesitate to work with your social worker or a trusted counselor so that you can manage your own emotions as you struggle to figure out how to address the baby's death with your Sunshine.

Caregivers who have a foster child die in their home will likely face increased scrutiny and public attention. When the foster care system is working well, even minor illnesses and injuries are reviewed by caseworkers to ensure that children remain safe. This is important because caseworkers need to be confident that a child's placement is not potentially dangerous. One way to ensure this is through procedures, paperwork, and reviews. It is easy to understand why when a child dies while in care, there is a lot of procedural scrutiny even if the death was not suspicious. However, this may be very unsettling for parents and sunshine children who may feel that their privacy is being compromised. It can also further feelings of self-doubt and guilt.

Additionally, some states require that the public is notified when a child dies while in care. This can mean that grieving families are held under a magnifying glass by the media. Obviously, such attention is incredibly disruptive to families and can leave parents and Sunshines feeling anxious, inadequate and attacked at a time when they are already overwhelmed by grief. For Sunshines, it can also result in conflict with peers. In these situations, it is important for families to find support from their social worker or another trusted adult. It is also critical that parents stay in close contact with their Sunshine's schools to protect peer relationships and identify any potential problems with other students.

Tragically, while kinship caregivers and foster families experience real grief when a baby dies, their grief is often "qualified" by those around them. In other words, their family, and friends may make statements such as, "At least your own kid is okay," or "Can you imagine how much worse it would be if it was one of your own kids?" Although likely offered as well-meaning encouragement, such words can be deeply wounding and invalidating.

Some parents may find that their loss is not even acknowledged at all. The experience of grief should never be qualified by anyone other than the person who is grieving. Of course, the truth is that kinship and foster families experience grief because they did their job well. Their grief is evidence that they gave their foster or kinship child exactly what they needed: the love of a family when their own could not provide it.

Because society does not always understand this truth and often undervalues the relationships that form between caregivers and the children in their care, many caregivers are excluded from rituals of grief that can help them mourn. For instance, while kinship caregivers may be involved in the child's funeral planning, many foster parents are not even invited to attend the service.

If you find that you are excluded from the rituals of grief that the infant's birth family has planned, I encourage you to find ways to memorialize the baby yourself. Gather your people together to remember the baby, organize a religious service or prayers for the baby, plan a butterfly release, or find a charity that you can support in honor of the child that you cared for. By finding tangible ways to express your love and grief, you will begin to comprehend its reality, find meaning in your loss, and understand that your sorrow is a legitimate response to losing someone you loved well.

Families Who Cannot Have More Children

For some, the death of their infant means that no other children will be added to their family. This may be due to maternal death or medical complications that make future pregnancies dangerous or impossible. For other families, the emotional or financial cost of pregnancy and loss is too great to try again. In these families the death marks the end of their hopes and dreams for a particular size family. Facing this truth is painful and it takes time to work through this added grief.

It is remarkable that most parents do eventually come to terms with shattered dreams and rebuild their lives in ways that are different but deeply meaningful. Their resilience, strength, and ability to embrace gratitude for what they have triumphs over their disappointment and sadness. Of course, these parents mourn, but they learn to find joy in the lives they have been given with their Sunshines. Some parents even report that their life was enriched by things that would not have been possible if it had gone according to their original plans.

When you wrestle with letting go of your dreams for your family, you model how to do this for your sunshine child. As you direct your focus away from growing your family and toward nurturing the one who is already with you, your Sunshine will also learn to accept what cannot be and to treasure what is. This is a valuable life lesson, and one that comes at great cost.

SECTION III: MOURNING WITH SUNSHINES

"Forgotten Grievers…Lonely Mourners."
-Katherine Fair Donnelly

"The influence of our families persists even beyond the time when we have close contact with them; indeed, it may persist even when family members are no longer living."
– Helen Rosen

Most mental health providers today recognize that children experience grief, but that was not always the case. In fact, many early child psychologists believed that children could not grieve until they had developed an understanding of death. Others, like Anna Freud, suggested that children are not able to mourn because they do not have a firm grasp of what is real and what is fantasy. Since many of her colleagues held similar beliefs, the leading psychologists of the day reasoned that children did not experience grief until they reached adolescence.

Psychology Nerd Moment: Anna Freud

Anna Freud was the daughter of the famous Sigmund Freud who developed psychoanalysis and, appallingly, psychoanalyzed Anna. Fortunately, our code of ethics would prohibit this today. Despite some of his more dubious methods, Sigmund's work helped to develop our current understanding of psychology. Although Anna is less well-known, her contributions to psychology were important. She continued to build on her father's ideas and applied them to children.

The practical result of such theorizing was that generations of bereaved children were left alone with their grief because the adults who cared for them did not believe that they were capable of grieving at all. In many families, the death of a family member was never discussed. In fact, in the 1980s, a survey of adults who lost siblings during childhood found that sixty-two percent had never talked about their sibling's death within their family. This is tragic because grief that is not discussed is often far more powerful and disruptive than grief that is shared with others.

Another potential consequence of denying the possibility of childhood grief was that children were excluded from rituals of grief that offer community and support. My own mother, for example, did not attend her grandfather's funeral because her parents believed that young children would only be confused and upset by such events. It is likely that you have similar stories within your own family.

The idea that so many generations of bereaved siblings had to bury their grief and suffer alone is beyond tragic and is a real stain on the history of child psychology. Thankfully, like all scientific fields, psychology is constantly experimenting, exploring, and evolving based on new information and that is precisely what happened in this case. Several influential leaders realized that childhood grief is a real and powerful experience. Thanks to their research, our theories about bereaved children changed as a result. We now recognize that the death of a family member deeply impacts even the youngest children.

Psychology Nerd Moment: The Pioneers of Childhood Grief	
Maria Nagy	Nagy suggested that, like all development, a child's understanding of death happens in phases. She felt that even very young children had some understanding of death and so they may experience grief. She reasoned that their experience would vary depending on their age and development.
Robert Furman	Furman suggested that most children have developed a basic understanding of death by the age of two. As a result, he believed that children aged two and older likely experience some form of grief, though it probably looks different from adult grief.
Myra Bluebond-Langner and team	Bluebond-Langner and a small group of researchers conducted a series of studies which showed that even very young, terminally ill children have a complex and realistic understanding of their own impending death. This means

	that even young children can understand death enough to grieve it.
John Bowlby	Bowlby studied attachment between children and their caregivers. He found that children as young as six months old experience distress when they are separated. He called this form of distress "grief."
Colin Murray Parkes	Parkes was John Bowlby's colleague. Together, they proposed a model of childhood bereavement that was based on Bowlby's Attachment Theory. They recognized that whether a child understood death, they experienced grief when they were separated from their caregiver. In other words, grief is primarily the result of broken attachment bonds and does not depend on understanding death.

Of course, you already know this because you are watching your own child grieve. Your sunshine child's attachment bonds with their sibling – bonds that would ordinarily provide emotional support, comfort, and wellbeing - have been irreversibly severed and so your child is grieving.

My goal in writing Section III of this book is to help you understand the nature of grief so that you can anticipate how it might impact your sunshine child over time. Unlike previous sections, while I offer practical advice whenever possible, this section is often more theoretical than practical, so I encourage you to take your time to process what you are reading. There is no rush. You have made it through the painful marathon of the first days after your baby's death. From this point forward, there are no time limits on your process of grieving. You and your sunshine child can choose your own pace.

CHAPTER FOURTEEN: A FAMILY IN MOURNING

"I keep describing grief as a house. I live in this house now. I just go from room to room. Paul and Carmella are here in the grief house too. We are healing together and alone."

- Christina Perri

After the initial shock of your baby's death and those early weeks that are full of "first-time-since-the-baby-died" milestones, your family will continue to navigate your grief together. While each member will journey through their sorrow differently, it can be helpful to understand the basic processes of grief.

Psychologists have proposed various models to help us understand the process of bereavement. I encourage you to view these as *descriptions* of grief, rather than *prescriptions*. In other words, a particular model might resonate with your own experience of grief, while another seems totally off-base.

Elizabeth Kubler-Ross

Of all the models of grief, Elizabeth Kubler-Ross' Stage Model of Grief is probably the most well-known. In fact, even if you do not know it, you have probably heard about certain aspects of her model. Kubler-Ross suggested that people grieve in five stages:

1. Denial

During this stage of grief, the mourner cannot accept and understand their loss, so they do not accept that it really happened. Instead, they might think things like, "She can't be dead. They made a mistake," or "It is all a dream. I will wake up and it will be over." While such thoughts do not make logical sense and are out of touch with the reality of the situation, they allow time to process pain and to come to terms with a new reality.

2. Anger

During the anger stage of grief, the grieving person is upset by any number of things. They may rage against God, their situation, someone they hold responsible for their loss, or even themselves. Angry grievers are generally irritable and easily provoked. In children, this may be misunderstood as acting out or misbehavior, so it is important to pay attention to what your child's actions may be telling you about their emotions.

3. Bargaining

When death is imminent, it is easy to understand how grieving families might cling to the hope that they could bargain away death with prayers to "take me instead." It is harder to understand how bargaining works after death has already occurred, because it can be more subtle. For example, someone might think, "If I just do this, then I will wake up and it will all be a dream," or "If I focus on my work, then the pain can all go away."

Some psychologists also think that our terrible "if only" games fall under the category of bargaining. These are the thoughts that keep you up at night: "If only I went to the hospital sooner;" "If only I hadn't eaten that;" "If only I didn't let them do an internal exam;" "If only I had listened to my body;" and on and on.

Bargaining allows us to believe that things are not as out of our control as they really are. Somehow, it is easier for us to accept that a baby died because of our failure than it is to come to terms with the fact that a baby died because the world is sometimes an unfair, dangerous place and people die for reasons that are completely out of our control.

4. Depression
This stage of grief involves a surrender to the profound sadness that death causes. Unlike clinical depression, which is a mental illness, the depression stage of grief involves negative emotions that are appropriate and expected in the context of death and loss. Individuals who are experiencing the depression phase of grief are likely to be fatigued, uninterested in usual activities, and profoundly unhappy.

5. Acceptance
For Kubler-Ross, this is the stage during which the griever accepts the new reality that death has created in their lives. They accept that there is no going back. Life will never be the same, but life will go on. During this stage, grievers take steps towards living their lives again, either by resuming their old lives with new insight or by seeking out an entirely new lifestyle. In a sense, this is the stage during which someone begins to move on.

Despite labeling each of these aspects of grief as stages, Kubler-Ross' model is not meant to be linear. Instead, one person in a family may first experience anger while another experiences denial. The time spent in each stage varies from person to person. Additionally, individuals may move back to stages they have already experienced. In other words, there is no order for movement between the stages.

For Kubler-Ross, the griever's goal is to reach acceptance of the death so that they can begin to move past their grief; however, for families that have lost an infant, acceptance may not be a reasonable goal. For families that have lost an infant, acceptance may not be a reasonable goal. Many families never accept the loss of a child. Instead, these families may find it more helpful to work towards the goal of finding meaning in their loss and purpose for their lives.

Bowlby & Parkes

John Bowlby and Colin Murray Parkes suggested that grief is a response to separation from someone we are attached to. This response happens in a series of phases. They are:

1. Numbness

Like Kubler-Ross' denial stage, a person who is experiencing the numbness stage is not yet able to feel the full emotional impact of their loss. Instead, they feel emotionally muted, numb, or disconnected from reality. To overcome this stage of grief, the griever must accept that their loved one has died and face their emotional response to this loss.

Psychology Nerd Moment: John Bowlby

You may not know John Bowlby by name, but as a parent of a Sunshine, you have most likely heard of his work. Bowlby developed a theory about how children bond with their parents called Attachment Theory. His work, and,

---

later that of Mary Ainsworth, is critical to our understanding of human development and child psychology. This is why he is mentioned repeatedly in this book.

However, Attachment Theory has been used to support Attachment Parenting which is a method of parenting with very strict guidelines that are meant to maximize parental attachment with their children. If you successfully utilized Attachment Parenting with your Sunshine, kudos to you, but don't worry if you have not lived up to Attachment Parenting standards! Scientifically based Attachment Theory was concerned with the emotional connections that formed as parents engaged with their child, rather than the specific acts during which these bonds were formed. In other words, it is important for a mother to feed her baby in a warm, responsive environment, but whether she bottle or breastfeeds is much less important. Which, when you think about it, sounds an awful lot like what Winnicott said about being a good enough, emotionally responsive parent.

1. Yearning and Searching

During this stage, the bereaved is trying to compensate for the void that their loved one's death creates in their life. They may seek solace from others in any or spend solitary time thinking about their loved one and clinging to whatever memories and reminders they have. Sometimes, grievers even imagine what it would be like if their loved one were still present in their lives.

2. Disorganization and Despair

This stage is marked by the realization that a loved one is truly dead and gone. The cost of this recognition is profound sadness and anger.

3. Reorganization

Grievers who have reached the reorganization stage of grief have begun to recognize that life goes on despite loss. They begin to hope again, experience fun and joy, and make meaning from their loss. Of course, they continue to miss their loved one, but their death is seen as part of a larger life story that is still being written.

Dual Process Model

One final model of grief is worth considering: the Dual Process Model of Coping with Bereavement. In this model, grief presents two types of demands:

1. Loss-oriented Demands

Loss-oriented demands are things the griever does that are related to the death of the baby. They include things like remembering the infant, breaking any emotional ties with the baby, and working through denial, sorrow and anger.

2. Restoration-oriented Demands

Restoration-oriented demands are things that the griever does as part of their daily routine that pushes them to move beyond the all-consuming thoughts of their loved one. These demands include things such as working, cooking, cleaning, hobbies and visiting friends and family.

Psychologists Stroebe and Schut, who developed the Dual Process Model, felt that grieving people must find a balance between these two types of demands so that they can both honor the dead and continue to engage in their own lives. This balancing act is normal and healthy.

Our response to the breaking of our relationship with our deceased loved one is a key aspect of both the Dual Process Model and Bowlby and Parkes' model. In fact, as pediatric palliative care doctor, Richard Goldstein, wrote, "Grief can be understood as an effort to maintain (attachment) bonds in the face of loss." The death of a baby creates unique challenges for families because each member has formed attachments to the infant in different ways - even before birth. For example, the act of carrying an unborn child inside of them, allows birth parents to learn things about their babies' personalities that help them to get to know their child and bond with them before they have even taken their first breath.[46] Unfortunately, when a baby dies close to the time of birth, other family members have not had the opportunity to get to know the baby in the same way. For other family members, their attachment is based primarily on their imagination, hopes and dreams of a future with the baby. Understandably, these are unique to everyone, which means that bonding – and therefore grief - will differ.

The roles that each family member plays in relation to the baby also influences what kinds of bonds are broken when a baby dies: mother-child, father-child, sibling-sibling. It may seem strange, but the truth is that before a baby is born, family members begin to shift their own identities so that they begin to see themselves in relation to the anticipated child. They identify themselves as mothers, fathers, and siblings well before the baby arrives. My daughter, for example, fully embraced her role as a big sister long before Noemi was born. She anticipated the things that she would someday teach her sister to do. In fact, even after Noemi's death, my Sunshine continued to say that she was a big sister.

Additionally, as has been discussed, children and adults tend to experience grief in different ways. With occasional exceptions, adults usually move through the stages and emotions of grief slowly over the period of days or weeks. Children, however, can seem to ricochet from one stage of grief to the next. My Sunshine would go from playing contentedly, to weeping as if the world would end and back to playing happily in a matter of minutes. This can be disconcerting for adults who forget that time is experienced differently when you are a child and that five minutes takes up a much bigger portion of a three-year-old's life than it does in an adult's life.

Raising Sunshine

Raising Sunshine

CHAPTER FIFTEEN: THE EMOTIONS OF GRIEF

"In times of grief and sorrow I will hold you and rock you and take your grief and make it my own. When you cry, I cry and when you hurt, I hurt. And together we will try to hold back the floods of tears and despair and make it through the potholed street of life."
- Nicholas Sparks

Although each member of the family will experience the emotions of grief differently, certain emotions occur almost universally. You can expect that both you and your Sunshine will experience sadness, anger, helplessness, anxiety, guilt, jealousy, and resentment. However, the intensity of each of these emotions and the times when you experience them will likely vary. By learning about each of these emotions, you can prepare yourself to handle them in both you and your sunshine child.

Sadness

Sorrow – or sadness - is the first emotion that people think of when they hear the word grief. It is often described as a deep ache or longing and regret that things are the way they are. In some people, this aching sensation is experienced as actual chest pain. Physically, people who are sorrowful tend to be fatigued, slower to respond and react, and less able to participate in enjoyable activities. They may eat more or less than usual and the food choices that they make tend to be less healthy.

There are many reasons that families who lose an infant are sad. Some are sorrowful that they will not be able to watch the infant grow. They grieve for the hopes, dreams, and plans that they had for their family and their child. Additionally, as we have discussed, the severing of attachment bonds causes feelings of sadness and loss.

Although sadness after the loss of an infant is beyond unpleasant, researchers think that it may help us to heal. By making us tired and slowing us down, sadness forces us to take the time to focus on our grief and rest from the busy pace of our normal lives. In doing so, sadness creates a space for us to process the baby's death. This helps us to accept the reality and finality of our loss. Feeling sad also allows us to acknowledge the bonds that we already had with the baby and to recognize the ways that the breaking of those bonds will impact us. It connects us with the baby and offers us a chance to express the love that we have for them. There is also evidence that feeling sorrow can help us to strengthen our communities by eliciting compassion from those around us. Finally, many psychologists believe that sadness is a motivator for change and growth, helping us to let go of what we once dreamed and to create new hopes and goals for our lives.

Sorrow after infant loss can be extreme. Dr. Richard Goldstein, whose work has focused on SIDS, has noted that grief after infant loss is often so intense that it would be considered abnormal in other situations. This can make it difficult for parents and their loved ones to know when their sadness has become more intense than normal and requires the help of a professional. The information in chapter seventeen can help you to tease out when sadness is appropriate and when you or your sunshine child may need professional support from healthcare providers.

There are some basic steps that you and your sunshine child can take to manage feelings of sadness.

1. Recognize your sadness
When we take time to recognize that we are feeling sad, we give ourselves vital information to use as we navigate our days. We can choose how our sadness will impact our behaviors, rather than letting our sorrow control us. By acknowledging our sadness, we give our minds the chance to influence our decisions with logic. This is important because the best choices we make

are the ones that make use of both the thinking and feeling areas of our brains.

You can help your sunshine child to recognize when they are feeling sad by making a point of identifying what emotions you are feeling yourself. By saying things like, "I was so happy when you gave me that kiss," or "I am feeling sad right now so I just want to sit here and do nothing," can help your child to label their feelings and encourage them to share these with you.

2. Create space for sorrow

Sadness is not inherently a problem, but it tends to become an issue when we ignore and neglect it. Author Joy Clarkson once said that emotions that are kept hidden away are like the captive wife in Jane Eyre. In that classic novel, a wealthy young man discovers that he has married a violent woman who is mentally ill. His solution is to lock her in the attic while continuing to live his life. However, when he tries to marry again, the wife escapes and burns down their mansion. Like the husband in the story, we may think that we can escape from the power of our emotions by avoiding and denying them, but in reality, the more we push them away, the more potent and out-of-control they become. Then, when they finally break free, they burn the whole house down! Her analogy is excellent because when we do not deal with our emotions, they really do become monstrous.

Of course, processing your sadness takes time, support, and solitude – all of which are in short supply for busy families. That is why it is so important that you and your sunshine child take the space you need to wrestle with your sorrow. One way to do this is to set aside certain times of the day when you can check in with yourself. Then, you can put your feelings on hold for a while and keep doing the things you need to do.

My "sadness times" were in the morning when I first woke up, in the shower, and during my Sunshine's nap. Knowing that I was going to have times when I could truly feel the depth of my sorrow allowed me to function and focus on living life with my Sunshine in between. Those times were like a valve, releasing the pressure of my grief so that I did not explode.

I encourage you to find time to let yourself feel your sadness. Get to know it because it will be traveling with you from now on. Right now, it can feel overwhelmingly bitter, but eventually, you will come to see its sweetness as an ongoing testament of your love for your baby. It takes time for you to become familiar enough with your sadness to see it that way, but once you do, you can pass this lesson along to your sunshine child.

3. Share your sadness

There is a proverb that says, "A sorrow shared is halved." When we share our sadness we find healing, but it can be so difficult! We worry about burdening those around us or appearing weak and ungrateful. Sometimes we think that no one will understand our sorrow or that people might treat us differently if they know what we are really feeling. However, by being honest about our sadness, we open channels of communication so that our other family members can share their own feelings more freely. At the same time, we gain support and comfort from their willingness to hear us and we feel less isolated as we realize that they empathize with our feelings. With the help of social media, modern society has evolved to value the projection of false images. Whether consciously or not, we are encouraged to always present ourselves as full of smiles, perfect and happy. True community, however, is built with vulnerability, revealed imperfections, and shared heartbreak.

Within the past six months both groups of women that I meet with regularly have discussed their desire to be part of a community that truly takes care of one another. Yet, the only way to build such a community is by being willing to share our feelings even when this requires us to be frighteningly open with one another. We must be willing to open ourselves to one another, trusting that our sadness will be received with tenderness and compassion.

4. Let your sunshine child see you sad

Your child is watching everything you do, even when you think they are not. I was reminded of this when I recently needed to use a chainsaw for the first time in my life. Although I could not figure out how to start it, my Sunshine correctly suggested that I pull back on one of the levers. As soon as I did, the saw whirred to life. I was surprised that she knew just what to do and, when I asked her about it, she casually replied, "Oh, I've seen Daddy do it when he is out cutting branches." My husband had never taught her how to use it, but my daughter observed and learned from him while she was playing nearby. [47]

In the same way, our children see us as we journey through grief and they gain knowledge from us. They learn to manage their own responses to their sadness as they watch us controlling the impact that our sorrow has on our behaviors. They discover how to give themselves space to grieve and time to live by seeing you do the same. They figure out how to express their sadness when you find ways to share yours. Ultimately, they come to tolerate their sadness with hope because they witness your hope even in your pain. So, let your sunshine child see you sad and let them witness the way that you are embracing and mastering your sadness. In doing so, you are teaching them to overcome their loss and reclaim their hope in living.

Anger

When a baby dies, it is natural for parents and siblings to feel anger. Sometimes this anger is a vague, nebulous sense of simmering rage. Other times, it is directed at a specific person or object. For example, family members may be angry at someone who they blame for their baby's death. Others become more sensitive to perceived insults, so they become irrationally upset when someone says or does "the wrong thing." There are also those who lash out at whoever happens to be around when their anger breaks loose. Like the proverbial owner who kicks their dog after a bad day, people around angry grievers bear the brunt of their anger. My own husband and father were like this after Noemi died. Tiny setbacks would send them into a rant that was completely out of proportion to the situation they were facing.[48]

If you or your sunshine child find that it is difficult to control your angry feelings after your baby's death, plan for how you will manage it. Anger is an enormously powerful emotion. While it has a bad reputation, when it is handled appropriately, it can be a potent motivation for change. In fact, psychologist Robert Biswas-Diener and author Todd Kashdan note that, "Altruism is often born from anger; when it comes to mobilizing other people and creating support for a cause, no emotion is stronger." Anger that is directed toward positive change can be a vital asset to our families and communities. Mourners who use their rage to address social issues, such as the disparity of healthcare in our society, the disproportionate risk for black babies, bias against LGBTQ+ families in the medical setting, and the lack of support for all grieving families, are often the ones who lead the movements that can bring about change. Their rage can be a powerful and valuable tool in bringing about needed societal transformation.

On the other hand, anger that is poorly managed can do a lot of damage. If you are concerned that you or your child is handling anger in a way that is harmful, there are steps you can take to manage it and minimize the damage it does to those around you.

1.   Tune into the moment that you start to feel anger stirring

The angrier we get, the more difficult it is for us to calm down and regain control of our feelings. Once we are consumed by anger, the parts of our brains that control rational thought shut down and we start to operate on pure emotion. Therefore, if you and your sunshine child can identify the physical and emotional signs that anger is building, you can intervene before your rational brain turns off.

Common things to look out for are:

✓ Angry thoughts (such as "She is so incompetent," or "Why is this taking forever?")

✓ Tense muscles (this can often be felt in the neck, shoulders, and jaw)

✓ Headache

✓ Rapid heart rate

✓ Clenched fists

✓ Raised voice

✓ Fast breathing

✓ Sweating

✓ Reddening face or blotchy neck

Take time to reflect on the way that your body feels when you are angry, then talk with your child about what happens in our bodies when we start to feel upset. By identifying these signs, you can catch anger before it spirals out of control and implement strategies to calm down.

2. Time Out

Once you or your sunshine child recognize that you are becoming angry, take a moment to problem solve and regroup. Like a movie director who sees a problem in a recorded scene, say "Cut!" Then take some time to figure out how to change course and move forward in a calmer, controlled way.

3. Choose How to Respond

Once you have put the brakes on your anger, you or your sunshine child can choose what to do next. Based on the situation, should you:

✓ **Focus on your thoughts**

We often assume that our emotions are a reaction to our environment, but the truth is that our emotions are really responses to *what we are telling ourselves* about that environment. If you think to yourself, "This person is incompetent. She can't even think outside of the box to help me!" the chances are good that you will eventually feel angry. If, on the other hand, you think about the same situation by telling yourself, "I am not getting what I need, but this person is trying her hardest. How can we work together to solve the problem?" you are much less likely to become angry.

Similarly, your biases impact the way you view the world. For example, if you are a person who values results over process, you are more likely to be angry when things get derailed because it delays or prevents you from reaching your goal. Alternatively, if you prioritize the process of getting to a particular result and the relationships that you build along the way, you will be more likely to see setbacks as opportunities for growth and not as obstacles in the way of reaching your goals. The way we view and interpret the world and the priorities we place on things play roles in our emotions.

✓ **Focus on your body**

Do you remember how you noticed that you were becoming angry? Most likely there were several physical signs that helped you to recognize what was happening. Our mind and body are woven together in such a way that a change in one creates a change in the other. In other words, when we experience anger, we are dealing with the activation of two separate but linked systems. I refer to them as "Angry Mind" and "Angry Body" when talking with children. Since it is possible to change either one and make a difference in the other, we can regain control of Angry

Mind by decreasing the physical expression of anger in Angry Body.

Appendix VII contains some relaxation activities that you and your sunshine child can use to soothe Angry Body. In addition to these exercises, it is possible to target the specific body parts that are being impacted by your anger. For example, if your shoulders tighten when you are angry, gently rolling your head from side to side can help. Similarly, if you recognize that you clench your fist or jaw when you are angry, consciously relaxing and opening those can be effective. The goal is to change what Angry Body is doing so that you allow Angry Mind to calm down.

✓ **Bring Out the Big Guns**

If you find that your anger has already passed the point that allows you to regain control in the ways above, there are still other ways that you can manage your anger and regain control. The following strategies can help you or your sunshine child to calm down enough to allow you to make conscious decisions about how to act and respond.

- Engage in strenuous physical activity – Angry Body is already feeling revved up, so engaging in activities that would have a similar physical effect can help to derail the progression of anger. Dancing, running, jumping jacks, and other high intensity activities produce physical feelings that are like those we feel in Angry Body. Doing these types of activities can trick Angry Mind into thinking that Angry Body is just Active Body. As a result, Angry Mind starts to calm down!

- Distract yourself – Focus on something that will force Angry Mind to stop thinking about whatever is fueling its anger. Listen to a song, read a book, try a new recipe, watch a movie, or listen to a podcast that will keep Angry Mind distracted and occupied, giving it the time and space it needs to cool down.

- Find a way to engage your senses – Sometimes, we can use our senses to redirect our focus off our anger. Strong physical sensations such as those triggered by sucking on a lemon, holding ice, taking a cold shower, listening to loud music, or smelling vinegar can be so overwhelming to our senses that Angry Mind is shocked out of its spiral out of control.

- Get out of there! – When nothing else works, leave the situation. Go for a walk, hang up on a frustrating phone call, take a break in a quiet room. Do whatever is necessary to get away from the source of the anger until Angry Mind and Angry Body have had a chance to chill.

When I was young, my family adopted an older couple who became like an additional set of grandparents to us. The man was a strong but gentle and calm person, his wife was a sweet and fiery woman. Once, when they were in their eighties, my mother asked how they were able to live together happily for so long and the man replied, "Whenever we fought, I would just leave and go on a long walk. I had some very long walks!" His technique was a good reminder that sometimes, we just need a little bit of space to calm down and regroup.

Managing anger can be difficult, but it is not impossible. The more you practice control, the easier it becomes, so encourage your sunshine child to use these techniques even when their anger is not overpowering. Practice with them so that you will both be prepared for the times when anger is more intense and threatens to take control.

Helplessness

When a baby dies, family members often feel helpless. One father reflected on his feelings of helplessness when he said, "I generally want to mend things – but a broken heart because of losing a child is a difficult thing to mend. It takes time and great patience...." In fact, so much of life after infant death demands herculean amounts of patience. Your routines are disrupted, your plans are thwarted, and everything about your life can feel unpredictable and chaotic. This is a recipe for helplessness and despair.

While it can be tempting to surrender to these feelings, doing so would obviously come at a great cost to you and your family. When people feel helpless, their physical and mental health suffers. One example of this was demonstrated in a study of mice who were put into a hopeless situation that caused them to develop what researchers called "learned helplessness."[49] [50] The study found that these mice had biological changes and developed behaviors that are like the ones that occur in humans who have Post Traumatic Stress Disorder (PTSD). For example, the mice showed problems with their appetite, disrupted sleep patterns and avoided anything related to their "traumatic" experience. However, when animals were given a sense of control over their experience, the symptoms decreased, and the mice seemed to become more resilient. If humans respond to hopeless situations in similar ways, we can surmise that two people could face identical traumas, but the person who feels that they have some control over their experience will fare better than the one who feels despair and hopelessness.

An additional finding suggested that animals who developed learned helplessness were more likely to seek out alcohol.[51] This caused the researchers to theorize that trauma and the helplessness that often accompanies it may cause brain changes that increase the likelihood of addiction and alcoholism.

Even in cases when feeling helpless in response to a trauma does not lead to life altering issues, it can have a negative impact on our lives. For example, people who feel little control over a traumatic experience are more likely to startle easily, be chronically stressed, and give up quickly when facing any future difficulties. Additionally, chronic stress has been found to cause multiple health related issues, including:

✓ Mental health problems

✓ Cognitive problems

✓ Stomach and digestive issues

✓ Headaches

✓ Cardiovascular problems and strokes

✓ Musculoskeletal pain

✓ Problems with Weight

✓ Fatigue

✓ Impaired Immune Function

Clearly, there are important reasons to minimize feelings of helplessness in yourself and your sunshine child. One way to do this is to develop an appreciation for the control that you do have over your life and the positive changes that you can make for your family even in the wake of your loss. At first, it might be difficult to identify things that you do have control over, but the more intentional you are about searching for them, the more you will recognize them. To get started, I encourage you and your sunshine child to make a list of the ways that each of you is helping your family to overcome the baby's death. Are you taking on additional responsibilities? Are you making a point of showing love to those around you? Are you truly listening to one another?

I suspect that you and your sunshine child do things every day that have an impact on the way that your family navigates their grief. By doing these "little," everyday things, you are using the power that you both have to bring about positive changes and healing in your family.

Another way to feel more in control of what your family is experiencing is to take an active role in decision making. Encourage everyone to participate in daily decisions about family life. These might range from simple things, like what to eat for dinner, all the way to major choices, such as whether to have a funeral for your baby. Share your own preferences and respect your sunshine child's opinions.

Although it can be hard to see in the moment, each of you has the potential to have an impact on your family's ultimate recovery from the death of your baby. It may not always be possible to recognize the positive differences you are making and the ways that you are growing until years later. Still, what you do each day impacts your tomorrows. While you could not control your baby's death, you can influence how your family moves forward through grief together.

Anxiety

When a baby dies, it is common to feel anxious about a variety of things. This is normal and is your mind's attempt to keep you safe.

Anxiety has a bad reputation, but it really is fundamentally a good emotion. When you feel fear in response to a potentially dangerous situation, that is a positive thing. In fact, if we were not evolutionarily predisposed to feel anxious when approached by a tiger, our species would likely not have survived!

One way to think about anxiety is to imagine it as a fire alarm. If the alarm goes off when there is smoke, it is doing its job to ensure your safety by allowing you to respond appropriately to a life-threatening situation. However, if the alarm malfunctions and goes off when there is no smoke, it is merely a distraction and a nuisance. If that same alarm starts going off all the time, for no apparent reason, then you have a big problem! Anxiety is the same. If it is alerting you to a real threat, then it is working as a valuable tool. On the other hand, once it starts to send off alarms when there is nothing to worry about, it is time for repairs.

It is especially important that parents do not let their faulty anxiety alarms run for too long, because parental anxiety has a big impact on children. Parents who are anxious are more likely to have kids who grow up to be depressed or anxious themselves. Some of this increased risk in children of anxious adults is genetic, some is because anxiety disrupts healthy parent-child bonding, and some is because of the limitations that anxious parents put on their children. Additionally, when we worry, we view the world negatively and focus on what is or could be wrong. Although we do not mean to, we pass this negative perspective onto our children, leaving them predisposed to mental health difficulties throughout their lives.

Fortunately, there are things that you and your sunshine child can do to manage anxiety so that alarms are triggered only when appropriate. Appendix VIII provides exercises that help to build anxiety management skills. For some parents and sunshine children, strengthening these skills is all it takes to get anxiety under control. Other times, people need help putting these skills into practice and making their anxiety alarm less sensitive. There are two ways to get this help: therapy and medication. In general, doctors prefer to try therapy first, adding medication only if therapy alone does not work. This is because studies have proven that talk therapy is the most effective way to treat anxiety.[52]

Even before Noemi's death, I was plagued by anxiety. In fact, it runs in my genes: my brother is a worrier, my parents are worriers, my grandparents were worriers, and I have heard enough stories about my distant ancestors to know that some of them were worriers, too! However, when Noemi died, my anxiety launched into overdrive. What was once a single alarm going off all the time became a 10-alarm fire alert.

In the past, I had reassured myself through research and seeking to understand the likelihood of my fears coming true. Statistics calmed me with the knowledge that my imagined worst-case scenarios were unlikely to occur. This approach lost its value after Noemi's death, which was a statistical improbability. In fact, at one point, I read that the chances of an infant dying as Noemi did were about one in 100,000. While I used to find comfort in the data that "proved" that my sunshine child's chances of dying in an accident were miniscule, I no longer found such data to be reassuring since I know that the risk of losing a child in an accident is about fifty-eight times greater than losing a baby in the way that Noemi died. I am sure that a statistician would cringe at my reasoning, but in my mind everything had changed. Nothing was safe enough because I now knew that my sunshine child could die. Child loss did not just happen to other people. It had happened to me, and I knew that it could happen again.

However, I also knew that I did not want my sunshine child's life to be limited by my own anxiety. Whenever I recognized that I was responding to something out of fear, I forced myself to take a step back and make a reasonable and informed choice that would balance my Sunshine's safety with her need for freedom and growth. However, by doing this, I was simply controlling the impact of my anxiety, not addressing it. I forced myself to allow her to do things, but I worried the whole time. This took a toll on me and left me on edge and ready to explode when anything went wrong. It also came at an unacceptable cost to my Sunshine. By not addressing the underlying thoughts that fueled my worries, I unwillingly taught my child to view the world as a potentially dangerous, hostile place. I began to hear my own worries reflected to me in her words and I saw my own hesitancy impeding her actions. Things needed to change.

Therapy alone was not enough for me because I could not access the skills I was learning when I was operating in emergency mode on a fulltime basis. I needed medication to balance the chemicals in my brain that kept my anxiety alert system alarming. As my alarm's sensitivity normalized, I became increasingly aware of my thoughts and able to choose whether to challenge them. Ultimately, I was able to do things that I had not even realized anxiety was keeping me from: traveling, participating in activities that involved heights, and hiking. As I gained control over my own worries, I was also able to help my Sunshine to recognize and overcome some of the negative thought patterns that she had absorbed from me.

Your journey out of anxiety will look different from mine. You and your sunshine child may or may not need therapy and/or medication. Perhaps practicing the exercises in Appendix VIII will be enough, or you will find sufficient comfort in calming physical exercises like yoga, Pilates or SoulCore.[53] However you ultimately manage your anxiety, remember that your choice to take control of it will have a lasting, positive impact on your sunshine child as you help them navigate their own fears and worries.

Guilt

When we grieve, it can be difficult to remember how strong we are. However, the truth is that the human mind is amazingly resilient and has developed remarkable ways of helping us through life's darkest times. We call these coping mechanisms. Many psychologists believe that guilt is one such coping mechanism. They suspect that our mind uses it to protect us from feelings of helplessness. Through their observations of human behavior, these experts conclude that we are so devastated by the idea that we cannot prevent tragedies that our mind convinces us that we did have at least some degree of control over the painful events. The unfortunate result is that we end up feeling that we bear some responsibility for our loss. Consequently, this coping mechanism does more harm than good, leaving us vulnerable to all kinds of physical and mental health problems.

To avoid such a scenario, you and your sunshine child need to be proactive about recognizing and managing your guilt. Identify what it is that you feel responsible for. Once you have done that, you can consider whether your feelings of guilt are appropriate. As a parent, you might consider asking yourself the following:

1. **What factors contributed to your loss and the decisions that you made? Were you:**

    ✓ Distracted?

    ✓ Tired?

    ✓ Afraid or anxious?

    ✓ Rushing?

    ✓ Driven by long-held hopes or dreams?

    ✓ Reminded of past traumas?

    ✓ Given poor advice?

    ✓ Suspicious of medical advice?

    ✓ Encountering a situation for the first time?

    ✓ Alone or without emotional support?

    ✓ Unaware of risks?

    ✓ Juggling limited financial resources?

    ✓ Battling an addiction that you had limited control over?

    ✓ Doing what you could to mitigate any risks you knew about?

    ✓ Concerned about your ability to care for your baby?

    ✓ Receiving medical care that was impacted by prejudice or geographic location?

    ✓ Was the hospital overcrowded or understaffed?

Each of these factors (and countless others) can play a role in infant death. Notice that, while you may wish that you had made different decisions, you were not acting in a vacuum. There are reasons that you made the decisions and choices that you did and, at most, you played only a small role in the constellation of factors that led to your baby's death. You can help your sunshine child to understand this too by teaching them to test their own feelings of guilt. Are their feelings based on a realistic understanding of what happened or on magical thinking? If there is any validity to their concerns, what is factored into them: age, fatigue, normal sibling rivalry, or something else?

2. **If a friend said that they felt guilty for the same reasons that you do, what would your response be to them?**

I suspect that if the tables were turned and you or your sunshine child were the ones offering reassurance and comfort to this friend, you would understand why they acted as they did and have compassion for them. In fact, it is likely that neither of you would hold them to the same standard that you are using to judge yourself. Why, then would you expect more from yourself than from others? I encourage you to be gentle with yourself and to think about your feelings of guilt in the same way that you would those of your friend, recognizing that none of us are perfect.

3. **Are you omnipotent?**

Of course, I know the answer to this question and so do you. Depending on their age, your sunshine child probably knows this, too. We are only human and we must therefore accept the limitations that all humans face. As human beings, we have limited knowledge, experience, time, resources, control, and patience. For this reason, any role that you or your sunshine child may have played in your baby's death is a single factor in a cascade of events.[54]

Maybe you did everything right and your baby still died, but most likely, there were things that you would choose to do differently if given the chance. Unfortunately, there are times when everything happens exactly the wrong way despite our best intentions. In these situations, it can help to remember all of the people who made the same choices you did but ended up with a different outcome. For example, how many parents did exactly what you did and still left the hospital with a healthy baby? They were no more responsible for birthing a healthy baby than you were for losing yours.

In our case, my husband and I did not realize that my water had broken for several hours. As a result, even though I knew that I had tested positive for Group B Strep, I did not receive IV antibiotics for part of my labor as is recommended. It is possible that Noemi may have lived if we had gone to the hospital sooner, but the truth is that many people labor at home for hours after their membranes rupture and they still hold healthy babies the next day. My baby died because I never had control over her living or dying. Accepting this fact is somewhat unsettling, but it helps me to let go of the guilt that I have sometimes felt about Noemi's death.

Letting go of guilt is certainly a difficult process, but it is essential to healing. Self-forgiveness will help to preserve both your physical and emotional health, freeing you to be fully present as you parent your Sunshine.

Jealousy and Resentment

There are numerous ways that families experience jealousy and resentment after a baby dies. Parents may envy others with healthy babies. Sunshine children might be jealous of a classmate who is playing with a baby sibling, or they might resent the attention that their parents are focusing on themselves as they grieve. Our society often condemns jealousy and resentment, perhaps because one of the tenets of several religious traditions is, "Thou shalt not envy." However, like any emotion, jealousy and resentment can be damaging when they are mishandled but are not intrinsically bad. Instead, the feeling of envy can help us to recognize what we value and desire. The challenge is to manage the feeling of envy so that it provides us with information but does not control us.

You and your sunshine child can take the following steps to deal with any jealousy or resentment in ways that will help you, rather than harm you:

1. Take time to consider why you are envious or resentful.

2. Accept your emotions and the simple fact that you feel them but remind yourself that our feelings do not always reflect reality.

3. Choose to believe that those around you are not hurting you intentionally by having a healthy baby or pregnancy.

4. Anticipate things like baby showers that might be difficult for you and take steps to protect yourself until you are feeling strong enough to deal with them.

5. Say "no" to activities and events that hurt too much.

6. Focus on building and maintaining relationships by minimizing the negative impacts that your resentment or envy could have on those around you.

It is natural for you and your sunshine child to feel jealous and resentful at times; however, the way that you respond to these feelings will have a significant impact on you and your relationships. With effort, you and your sunshine child can learn to recognize what your envy and resentment is teaching you while simultaneously making sure that your feelings do not interfere with your ability to connect with those around you.

Raising Sunshine

Raising Sunshine

CHAPTER SIXTEEN: UNDERSTANDING YOUR SUNSHINE'S GRIEF

"There is a sacredness in tears. They are not the mark of weakness, but of power. They speak more eloquently than ten thousand tongues. They are the messengers of overwhelming grieve, of deep contrition and unspeakable love."
- Washington Irving

As parents, we instinctively try to fix things for our children. Many of our actions are driven by our goal to keep our little ones safe and happy. When they hurt, we suffer with them and we willingly sacrifice almost anything to make things better for them. It goes without saying, however, that pain and suffering are inevitable in life, and it is impossible to shield our sunshine children from them. However, because we can understand their pain, we can journey with them and be ready to help and support them in whatever ways we can.

Walking with our sunshine children as they grieve is not an easy task. For one thing, all individuals grieve in unique ways, and the different responses Sunshine's have can be perplexing. Additionally, your sunshine child's needs may be very different from your own, making it difficult to adequately meet both. When you feel discouraged in your parenting, know that any effort you make to understand what your sunshine child is going through helps to build your ability to support them as they survive this struggle.

The Difficulties of Being a Sunshine Child

Sunshine children face several unique challenges. Perhaps, the biggest of these is also the one you have the most control over: you. As was discussed in Section II, your ability to navigate your own loss directly impacts your availability to your child. If your own grief limits or prevents you from being a present and consistent parent, your sunshine child will grieve a double loss - the loss of their sibling and the loss of the parent they have known. That is why it is critical that you invest in your own healing. As Katherine Donnelly wrote, this is particularly important because children often interpret changes in parental availability and behavior as indications that their parents love for them has changed. No loving parent would want their child to think that they are less loved, especially in the midst of grief.

The second challenge that faces grieving sunshine children is also one that you have some level of control over. The aftermath of infant death leaves disrupted lives. Some families physically move away from reminders of their lost hopes and dreams. Other families change the way they function as a unit. Such changes may be necessary; however, they can be upsetting to a child whose world has suddenly become unpredictable and insecure. Whenever possible, try not to make dramatic changes immediately following your baby's death. When change is necessary, take time to prepare your child and try to maintain routines and minimize disruptions as much as possible.

Another challenge for Sunshines is that grieving siblings often lack social support. When a child experiences the death of a close family member, such as a parent, there is usually an outpouring of assistance from friends and family. However, this safety net does not always materialize when a child loses a sibling, particularly when that sibling is an infant. This may be because family and friends are focused on helping the parents through their disabling grief. Other times, the lack of support for sunshine children is the result of incorrect assumptions that the loss of an infant sibling is somehow less traumatic than other losses. Whatever the cause, the result is that many sunshine children navigate their sibling's death without the support that they would ordinarily have in times of grief. Knowing that your child may not have the social support that they need can motivate you to be intentional about creating a community for them. Encourage relationships with supportive people outside of your home and invite others into your family's grief through events like funerals and memorial walks. Additionally, consider having your child attend a support group at a local grief center or a summer camp that focuses on grieving siblings.

Sunshine children may struggle because, while they are experiencing intense grief of their own, they also feel pressured to be strong for their parents. Sometimes this pressure is applied directly, such as when well-meaning adults try to comfort sunshine children by saying things like, "You must be strong for mommy. You don't want her to be upset if she sees you so sad." Other times, the sunshine children themselves feel compelled to protect their parents. In one survey, up to a third of siblings said they felt that they needed to comfort or care for a parent. To do this, these children often hid their own grief, making it almost impossible to heal themselves. For this reason, it is important for parents to tell their sunshine children that it is okay for them to be sad and to reassure them that you want them to be open with you about their emotions. It should be very clear that, while Sunshines may offer you comfort and happiness, you are the caregiver and you are there to support them.

Sunshine children face the challenges of grief against the backdrop of a common disadvantage: they have limited life experiences and understanding. Unlike adults who have had opportunities to develop skills that help them deal with difficulties, sunshine children often have few experiences to draw on as they struggle to figure out how to respond to their loss. This means that they depend heavily on adult role-models to help them to navigate their sibling's death. As a result, you can play a big role in how your sunshine child responds to their grief, simply by showing them how you grieve and welcoming them to find healthy ways of expressing their emotions.

Additionally, most sunshine children do not fully comprehend death. If we are honest, does anyone? But sunshine children are at a greater disadvantage because their brains are not developmentally ready to truly understand the finality of death. With time, their comprehension will expand and mature as they find meaning in their loss. This process may require that they circle back to specific memories or ideas again and again as they try to process their experiences with newly acquired knowledge.

In all losses, symptoms of grief are frequently intense. In fact, if someone experienced them while not in the midst of grieving, they might be identified as having a mental or physical illness. However, in the context of infant death, these symptoms are to be expected. Nevertheless, if anything about how your family is coping with your baby's death concerns you, do not hesitate to reach out to a licensed medical or mental health provider for advice.

Expected Behaviors

While adults are generally able to identify and talk about their emotions, children have more trouble with this. Consequently, they tend to "show" their emotions through behavior. Helen Rosen suggested that grieving children display four different types of behavior:

1. Behaviors that help children accept their loss (acceptance behaviors)

2. Behaviors that help children stop doing things that are "no longer appropriate" because of the death (ending behaviors)

3. Behaviors that help children to manage intense emotions and feelings (emotion behaviors)

4. Behaviors that help children to feel safe and in control of their life (control behaviors)

While many of these behaviors can be difficult for parents to tolerate, they are all common in children who have lost a sibling. However, two specific types of behaviors associated with infant loss deserve more attention. The first is the tendency for children to either withdraw or act out when they are distressed. Many children handle negative emotions by misbehaving or pulling away from those around them. Behavior, then, can be a good indication of what children are feeling. For this reason, child therapists are trained to recognize acting out and withdrawal behaviors instead of focusing on the emotions that children report.

Common Symptoms of Grief

Behavioral Symptoms	<ul><li>Withdrawal</li><li>Irritability</li><li>Acting Out</li><li>Poor Concentration</li><li>School/Work Difficulties</li><li>Nervous Habits (Like Nail Biting or Skin Picking)</li><li>Sleep Difficulties</li><li>Increased or Decreased Appetite</li><li>Regressed Behaviors (like bedwetting after being fully trained)</li><li>Driving Accidents</li></ul>
Cognitive/Emotional Symptoms	<ul><li>Sadness</li><li>Loss of Interest</li><li>Unwanted or Distressing Thoughts</li><li>Nightmares</li><li>Altered Sense of Reality</li><li>Preoccupation with the Loss</li><li>Confusion</li><li>Wishing to die[55]</li><li>New or Worsening Mental Illness</li></ul>

	• Addiction
Physical Symptoms	• Pain (Stomach Aches, Headaches, Tight Muscles, etc.)
	• Sleep Disturbances
	• Fatigue
	• Weakened Immune System (Resulting in Repeated Colds, Ear Infections, etc.)
	• New or Worsened Chronic Illness
	• Feeling Symptoms Related to How the Baby Died (Like Chest Pain)

Generally speaking, children want to please adults. They also fundamentally desire love and respect. Therefore, it is safe to assume that a sunshine child who is getting into a lot of "trouble" is having difficulty managing overwhelming, negative emotions. The same is true of sunshine children who withdraw and appear to be less interested and engaged in the lives that they once enjoyed. While it can be difficult to live with a withdrawn or misbehaving sunshine child, it can help to know that these behaviors are the result of their distress. This understanding provides you with the opportunity to help your sunshine child to figure out ways to manage their emotions more effectively.

Some sunshine children are easy to teach. They respond to a simple question like, "I can see that you are really upset about something, can you tell me what is wrong?" Others require more persistence and creativity. You may need to be less direct as you help them explore ways to express themselves. By addressing the root of your child's behaviors rather than trying to change the behaviors through external control and discipline, you will ultimately be much more effective. You will also find that your bond with your child is deepened as you work through their emotions together.

A second behavioral issue in grieving children is that many Sunshines need to process their loss repeatedly over time. This can be exhausting, boring and even emotionally painful for grieving parents. As noted previously, grief is dealt with in different ways and often the age of the child impacts their experience of grief. Younger children tend to learn and understand things best through play, so you may find that your young sunshine child plays the same game repeatedly. Their play might clearly reflect details of the baby's death, or it may be more symbolic. For example, our sunshine daughter constantly played two imaginative games after Noemi died. In the first, she pretended that she was a baby who was in danger and needed me to save her. This game was obviously linked to Noemi's death and, thankfully, our friends understood this because it was an excessively morbid game for someone her age. The second game (which she played for more than three years) was not directly linked to her sister's death but involved reenacting the movie that she watched when she needed to "escape" from our grieving family. Her games stood out to me as a school psychologist because she played them compulsively, constantly, and in a specific way. If anyone deviated from the script that she had created, she became very upset. Gradually, however, as she began to work through her emotions about her sister's death, her play became more flexible and she was able to incorporate changes into her play routine.

Types of Grief Behaviors

Acceptance Behavior	Ending Behaviors	Emotion Behaviors	Control Behaviors
Talking About the Baby	Not Talking About the Baby all the Time	Avoiding Things Associated with Babies or Death	Insisting on Rigid Routines
Asking Questions	Abandoning Dreams of What They Would Do with the Baby	Crying	Compulsive Actions
Acting Out the Death through Imaginative Play	Writing To the Baby Instead of Singing to Him or Her	Acting Out (Screaming, Disobeying, Hitting, etc.)	Double Checking Everything
Memorializing the Baby's Life		Regressive Behaviors (Disrupted Sleep or toileting, etc.)	Not Wanting to Leave Mom and Dad
Connecting with Other Grieving Children		Asking for Reassurance	Repetitive Play
		Withdrawing From Friends	Obsessing Over School Work
		Difficulty Focusing	Manipulating Situations

Older children are less likely to process their grief through imaginative play but may instead need to repeatedly discuss their grief or create things that express their emotions. In fact, in a paper that was written to help school counselors treat bereaved siblings, David Balk wrote, "Retelling the story seems to be a needed source of healing in the process of grief resolution."

Processing grief is important work. As Rosen said, "It is generally believed that when there is a loss of a significant person in the life of a child, the expression of feelings – guilt, anger, anxiety – is helpful and should be allowed and encouraged." Additionally, mental health professionals believe that talking about an event not only helps children to understand it, but it also helps them to believe it really happened. Therefore, talking about their loss helps sunshine children to experience their grief, accept their loss and incorporate it into their understanding of who they are. These things are all essential to healing.

Sadly, in a study of bereaved siblings from my generation, seventy-six percent reported that they were not able to talk with anyone about how they felt when their sibling died.[56] This same study found that sixty-two percent of siblings said that they did not even discuss their sibling's death with their families. Isn't that tragic?

Despite the importance of allowing children to process their grief, sunshine children of all ages may benefit from establishing some boundaries related to when and where it is appropriate to do so. Otherwise, their activities might distress other children and negatively impact their social interactions. While it is important that your sunshine child does not feel silenced, you can talk with your child about appropriate settings for doing their grief work. You can simultaneously reinforce how important this work is and that you are proud of them for facing their grief. By helping them to establish boundaries in this way, you teach your Sunshine that their grief is not something to hide but something to manage.[57]

The Social Impact of Childhood Grief

Even though their sibling was a part of their lives for only a brief time, sunshine children often find that the death of their brother or sister impacts every area of life, including their interactions with peers. Both parents and teachers report that bereaved siblings have more challenges with social interactions and tend to be more withdrawn for up to two years after their sibling's death. Sunshine children themselves are often aware that their relationships are suffering, and they feel disconnected from their peers. Additionally, Sunshines often seem to struggle to fit in.

Part of the reason that sunshine children feel isolated is probably because grief makes them less interested in social activities. Primarily though, this sense of separateness is triggered by peer responses (or lack of responses) to the baby's death. Often, sunshine children's friends and classmates do not know how to talk with someone who is grieving. They may do things that cause sunshine children to feel alienated like saying "the wrong thing," trying to cheer them up, or being impatient with the sunshine child's grief and wanting them to "just get over it." These responses are invalidating and can cause sunshine children to pull away from their peers. Probably for this reason, school-aged sunshine children report that when their friends and classmates acknowledge their loss, they feel better because their sorrow is seen and heard. On the flip side, when peers avoid talking about their sibling's death, sunshine children feel alone.

Although it is helpful for friends and important adults to talk about their sibling's death, sunshine children do not always know how to navigate these conversations. Author Jodi Picoult highlighted the uncertainty of these situations when she wrote in one novel: "If you have a sister and she dies, do you stop saying you have one? Or are you always a sister, even when the other half of the equation is gone?"[58] A real grieving sibling individual talked about the difficulty that she had in deciding whether to mention her sibling's death in casual conversations: "It is always weird when people ask if I am an only child because you don't want to get awkward, but at the same time you don't want to lie."

Children quickly learn that some people respond appropriately and supportively when they talk about their loss, but others respond in ways that are hurtful or dismissive. Peers are not the only ones who are insensitive; there have been heartbreaking stories of teachers who disciplined students who chose to include their deceased sibling on family-tree projects. You can play a role in helping your sunshine child to determine when sharing will be beneficial and when it may be counterproductive. This can help them to feel more confident and prepared for social interactions.

In my experience, discerning when to talk about sibling death with friends and strangers is an ongoing process for my sunshine daughter. This is largely because social situations and expectations change over time, but it also reflects my Sunshine's own changing needs. For example, when Noemi first died, our sunshine child was very open about her grief and her friends were overwhelmingly supportive and comforting, even though many of them were too young to truly understand what had happened. Over time, she became more ambivalent about talking about her sister with her teachers and peers. Partly, this was because some of her friends' parents were uncomfortable when they overheard her talking about Noemi's death and they tried to redirect the conversation. However, as she has grown and thrived in her life since Noemi's death, she has less need to share about her loss and she does not always want people to know her as "the girl who lost her sister."

While I have been impressed by the way my Sunshine has navigated the social aspects of her loss, like any child, she has not always navigated them in the way that social etiquette columnists would suggest. In fact, some of her approaches have been extremely embarrassing for her parents! The most obvious example of this happened a few weeks after Noemi died. To assuage my mother's guilt over my Sunshine's grief, I did everything I could to make her

Halloween perfect that year. My sunshine daughter had a great costume, I spent hours (and most of my finger cartilage) carving Disney's Princess Belle into her pumpkin, and we were excited to go trick-or-treating as a little family. At first, nothing was amiss. We followed our Sunshine from door to door and she politely received her candy. However, about half-way through the evening, she asked us to stay on the sidewalk while she went up to a door alone. We watched as she rang the doorbell, smiled at the woman who opened the door, and declared, "Trick or treat! My baby died. Can I take two?" Of course, the woman did not know what to say and looked down the sidewalk to where we were standing wearing expressions of shock and dismay. We quickly intervened and, a few moments later, two very embarrassed parents and one very satisfied child walked away from the house with an impressive bounty of candy! The obvious chocolate rewards that resulted from her unexpected plea for sympathy made it difficult for our sunshine daughter to understand why she was instructed to exclude her sister's death from her future trick-or-treat greetings.

Embarrassing and uncomfortable moments like the one just described have taught me that people are often very kind and generous when these situations are approached with openness and honesty. Most of the time, people recognize that you and your sunshine child are living in uncharted territory, and they are willing to overlook your child's minor faux pas as they focus on building connections with you. In fact, some of our most awkward moments have led other people to share their own stories of loss and helped us to form new and meaningful connections that have been healing for both them and us. In a way, it seems that when the masks we show the world are stripped away, those around us willingly remove their own masks, enabling us to relate to one another as vulnerable human beings. This is an incredibly beautiful thing.

Age Dependent Aspects of Grief

While sunshine children of all ages grieve, age influences their experiences and expressions of it. It seems obvious that a two-year old's grief looks very different from that of a nine-year old. However, how a Sunshine grieves depends more on their level of development than on their chronological age; so if your sunshine child is precocious, do not be surprised if their grief seems like that of an older child. On the other hand, if your sunshine child is developing at a slower pace, their way of grieving will reflect this. Nevertheless, sunshine children generally respond to grief in predictable ways at certain ages.

The following pages break down grief behaviors and experiences by age so that you can have a clearer sense of what to expect from your child.

Under Age Two

It goes without saying that infants and young toddlers have a limited understanding of death. Their rudimentary language comprehension makes it more difficult for them to communicate their feelings. It also makes it hard for you to explain things to them. At this age, sunshine children tend to grieve because they sense separation or abandonment. Primarily, they are responding to your emotional responses and resulting changes in your ability to be present with them.

You can help very young children by focusing on including memories of their sibling into your family life. You can also help them to process any emotions through art and play. Most importantly though, babies and toddlers need you to maintain familiar routines, provide reassurance through structure, and offer them lots of love and affection.

Signs of Grief in Infants and Toddlers

✓ More crying than usual
✓ Fussiness

✓ Clinging behaviors

✓ Evidence of separation anxiety[59]

✓ Regression[60]

Two to Six

Preschool and early elementary-aged children have trouble understanding the finality of death. They tend to think of death as being reversible or temporary. It is developmentally normal for children at this age to use magical thinking in daily life, so their understanding of the death can involve some "magical," unrealistic ideas. For example, it is common for children at this stage of development to believe that their own negative thoughts caused the baby to die.

Young children thrive on structure and predictability, but infant death is often disruptive. An important way to help children in this age range is to reestablish the comfort of routines as quickly as possible. You should also focus on managing your own grief so that you are emotionally available to your child.

Signs of Grief in Preschool and Early-School Aged Children

- ✓ Sadness
- ✓ Anger
- ✓ Aggression
- ✓ Regression
- ✓ Nightmares
- ✓ Disobedience
- ✓ Separation Anxiety
- ✓ Fear of their own death
- ✓ Acting out behaviors[61]

Six to Nine

School-age children gradually develop an understanding that death is forever. Nonetheless, they still retain some aspects of magical thinking and tend to think of death as a person or a thing rather than as a state of being. This may mean that they think of it as something that can be escaped or avoided.

While school-age children have a greater capacity to understand sibling death than younger children do, they often continue to misinterpret certain aspects of death. Many consider themselves to be responsible for their sibling's death and feel guilty as a result. As was discussed previously, one way to help your sunshine child is to figure out what specific things your child understands about death and gently correct their misconceptions so that they do not erroneously assign blame to themselves.

Signs of Grief in Children Between the Ages of Six and Nine

- ✓ Guilt
- ✓ Phobias[62]
- ✓ Fear of their own death
- ✓ Caregiving behaviors (for example, trying to care for their parents)
- ✓ Possessiveness of Parents
- ✓ Aggression
- ✓ Regression
- ✓ Physical complaints (stomach or headache, etc.)
- ✓ Difficulty concentrating
- ✓ Poor school performance
- ✓ Social difficulties/withdrawal
- ✓ Acting out behaviors
- ✓ Difficulty expressing feelings

Nine to Twelve

Young adolescents usually understand that death is final, but they may have difficulty imagining their own death or that of someone they love. This is partly because they think concretely and may struggle with more abstract concepts and ideas. At this age, sunshine children might ask questions about the "mechanics of death" (how it happens, what does it look like, what happens to a body after it is buried, etc.). This reflects their concrete thinking and is one way that they are trying to make sense of their loss.

At this age, sunshine children are acutely aware of their parents' grief. Witnessing their parents' sorrow increases their own sadness and can make it harder for them to continue to grow towards independence, which is an essential milestone for this age group.

Signs of Grief in Children Between the Ages of Nine and Twelve

✓ Phobias

✓ Sadness

✓ Anger

✓ Guilt

✓ Difficulty concentrating

✓ Poor school performance

✓ Social difficulties/withdrawal

✓ Defiant or acting out behaviors

✓ Aggression

✓ Physical complaints (stomach or headache, etc.)

Twelve and Above

Older adolescents and teenagers often recognize that death is permanent, universal, and inevitable. They are also able to grapple with abstract and philosophical thoughts about death so they can think about it in a more complex way. It has been said that teenagers have an almost adult understanding of death but lack the coping skills to deal with it. This is important to keep in mind as you face their frustrating behaviors that seem so out of sync with your teen's reasoning ability.

Even in the best of circumstances, many teenagers avoid talking about their feelings with their caregivers. For grieving teens, the motivation to withhold information about themselves from their parents sometimes stems from a desire to protect their loved ones who are grieving themselves. At the same time, teenagers are more likely to turn to their peers for support. This shift reflects their growing independence.

Because they hide their emotions, it can seem like teenaged sunshine children have moved on from their loss. However, for many, their grief is long-lasting. In fact, more than half of the teenagers participating in one survey reported feeling that they would never feel better again. It is important to be sensitive to the fact that although your teenager seems "okay," they may be dealing with many difficult emotions that are lying under the surface. These hidden feelings can influence their decision making and behavior.

Although teens may not choose to engage in conversations about their loss, they frequently report that they appreciate knowing that someone is willing to listen and talk with them. Teen siblings also report a wish that people would avoid trying to change how they are feeling; they do not want to be changed, just understood. Consequently, they require the space to wrestle with emotions that can be painful and uncomfortable for their parents to witness.

While the symptoms of grief can be overwhelming and scary to parents, it is important to remember that most children will respond to and overcome their grief in normal and healthy ways. Some children, however, need additional help to navigate their journey through grief. The next chapter will address signs that your Sunshine's grief is more extreme than is usual and that they may benefit from professional help.

Signs of Grief in Teenagers

- ✓ Sadness/Depression
- ✓ Fear
- ✓ Anger
- ✓ Shock
- ✓ Confusion
- ✓ Numbness
- ✓ Relief
- ✓ Guilt
- ✓ Defiant behaviors
- ✓ Aggression
- ✓ Trouble sharing their emotions
- ✓ Difficulty concentrating
- ✓ Poor school performance
- ✓ Low motivation
- ✓ Risk taking behaviors
- ✓ Increased or new sexual activity
- ✓ Substance abuse
- ✓ Possessiveness
- ✓ Physical complaints (stomach or headache, etc.)
- ✓ Social difficulty/altered relationships
- ✓ Loneliness
- ✓ Questioning of previously held assumptions about the world and their beliefs
- ✓ Suicidality[63]

Raising Sunshine

CHAPTER SEVENTEEN: WHEN ITS NOT "JUST GRIEF"

"My dark days made me stronger. Or maybe I am already strong, and they made me prove it."

- Emery Lord

The death of an infant sibling is a traumatic event for sunshine children. In fact, it can be so upsetting that during the early stages of grief, it is often difficult to determine what is normal and what is "more than normal." Hopefully, this chapter will help you to recognize warning signs that your sunshine child is experiencing "more than normal" grief. However, if you are concerned about them, do not hesitate to seek help from a professional who has worked with grieving patients. Such professionals are equipped to help you determine whether your sunshine child might benefit from additional therapeutic support or medication.

Watch Out For:

- Intense grief that does not lessen over time (by six months, your child should start to feel their grief less severely)

- Grief that causes significant difficulties in any area of life

- Preoccupation with the loss that does not lessen over time

- Difficulty accepting the reality of the death after the first few weeks

- Disruptive attempts to avoid reminders of the loss

- Intense and lasting anxiety about being separated from a parent

- Feeling life is meaningless

- Less interest in things that they used to enjoy

- Feelings of sadness that don't gradually ease

- Acting out behaviors that continue over time

- Persistently low self-esteem or feelings of guilt

- Disruptions to important relationships

- Risk taking behaviors (unprotected sex, drugs, alcohol, fast driving, etc.)

- Substance use and abuse

- Anything that concerns you or doesn't feel right

Trauma Reactions

Because infant death is a traumatic event, sunshine children can experience trauma reactions. Like survivors of other types of trauma, these sunshine children may think about the baby constantly, experience upsetting dreams about the baby, repeatedly envision the moment they learned about the baby's death, or feel overwhelmed by anxiety when something reminds them of the baby. Your Sunshine may also display trauma reactions related to any life-threatening pregnancy or delivery complications that you yourself may have faced.

On their own, these symptoms of trauma are not unusual and do not necessarily mean that your sunshine child has a trauma related mental health issue. However, if the intensity of the symptoms does not diminish over time and if these symptoms interfere with their ability to live their life, it is possible that they are experiencing a trauma disorder. The best known of these is Post Traumatic Stress Disorder (PTSD), a diagnosis which requires symptoms to last for at least a month. If symptoms have been going on for less than a month, then your child might meet the criteria for an Acute Stress Disorder.

While only a trained clinician can diagnose either PTSD or Acute Stress Disorder, the criteria used to make such a determination are listed in the table entitled, *Is It PTSD*.[64] If your sunshine child is experiencing several of these symptoms, it is probably worth talking to your child's primary care provider or a mental health professional. It is not necessary for a child to experience all of the symptoms listed in the table to be diagnosed with one of these trauma disorders.

Even if you do not think that your sunshine child's symptoms fit a particular diagnosis, if any symptoms are particularly troubling, do not hesitate to seek help. You should also consult a professional if your sunshine child is using alcohol or other substances as a means of self-treatment or if you are concerned that your child may be suicidal.

If a clinician determines that your sunshine child does have a trauma related disorder, they can help to develop an action plan to conquer it. While medication is sometimes needed, the primary treatment for these disorders is therapy. This may include Cognitive Behavior Therapy (CBT), Eye Movement Desensitization and Reprocessing (EMDR), or exposure therapy. These types of therapies work differently to address thoughts and responses to trauma.

CBT helps your sunshine child to alter their thoughts and behaviors in ways that influence their emotions. EMDR uses repetitive side-to-side eye movement to help your sunshine child react less intensely to the trauma. This might sound a bit like snake oil, and in fact, it is not completely clear why EMDR works. The psychologist who first used it, Francine Shapiro, theorized that it helped the different parts of the brain make connections and store traumatic memories in a healthy way rather than in the fragmented way that traumas are often stored. Whether or not this is *why* EMDR works, research has repeatedly demonstrated that it *does* work. Exposure therapy involves helping your sunshine child to focus on the details of their traumatic memories while simultaneously working with a therapist to use relaxation skills that minimize their emotional responses to these memories. Over time, as your sunshine child is exposed to their trauma related memories, the amount of anxiety that the memories cause will lessen.

Is It PTSD?	
Does your sunshine child have any of these symptoms:	• Repeating memories of their loss that upset them • Distressing dreams • Flashbacks (they feel like they are reliving their loss) • Feeling out of touch with reality • Distressed by reminders of their loss • Physical responses to things related to their loss (sweating, rapid heart rate, nausea, etc.)
Do they...	• Avoid thoughts and feelings related to their loss • Avoid things that remind them of their loss
Are they experiencing at least two of the following...	• Unable to remember important things about the loss • Negative thoughts and expectations about themselves and the world

	• Unfairly blame themselves or someone else for the baby's death
	• Negative emotions that don't let up
	• Less interest in things they used to enjoy doing
	• Feeling isolated or separated from those around them
	• Unable to experience emotions that make them feel good
Do they have two or more of the following…	• Irritability or volatile emotions
	• Reckless and dangerous behaviors
	• Constantly on alert in case something goes wrong
	• Startle easily
	• Trouble focusing
	• Problems with sleep
Have these symptoms lasted for…	• One month or less (Acute Stress Disorder)
	• More than one month (PTSD)

Depression

While it is normal to be sad after a baby dies, sunshine children are at an increased risk of depression, so it is especially important to pay attention if their sadness is intense and lasting. Unfortunately, it is often challenging to distinguish between normal grief and depression. In fact, this distinction is so difficult that the American Psychiatric Association has classified some aspects of grief as "Conditions for Further Study" because of our limited understanding of grief and the way that it impacts mental health.

Considering this, if you have any concerns about your sunshine child's level of sadness, I strongly suggest that you seek advice from a licensed mental health professional. They are trained to recognize symptoms of depression that you might miss. Even if your Sunshine does not meet the criteria for depression, a professional can offer suggestions for helping them through their sadness.

You should not hesitate to seek advice in any of the following situations:

- ✓ Your sunshine child's sadness is concerning to you or those around you

- ✓ Their sadness is constant rather than lessening over time or coming in waves and then diminishing

- ✓ Feelings of sadness, anger or guilt are taking over your sunshine child's life

If the provider you consult with determines that your sunshine child is depressed, they will help you to figure out how to treat this illness. In most cases, the provider will suggest some combination of counseling and medication.

Unfortunately, finding a mental health practitioner who sees children can be difficult, particularly if you are limited to providers who accept your insurance. Your sunshine child's pediatrician can offer recommendations for local providers. Additionally, your health insurance can often provide you with a list of practitioners on their provider list. Another option is to call SAMHSA's National Hotline Referral Center at 1-800-662-HELP (4357). Alternatively, consider contacting a psychology training program at a university near you. These sometimes offer visits with supervised trainees at significantly reduced rates. If cost is an issue for you, know that many therapists will work on a sliding scale for uninsured or out-of-network clients, so feel free to ask about this option if you are having trouble finding someone within your insurance network.

Substance Use

Older sunshine children may be at risk of substance abuse. As mentioned previously, stress and grief cause people to be more likely to use and misuse substances. Negative emotions can trigger us to desire mind-altering substances. Additionally, they can make it more difficult to control our intake of these substances. In fact, brain imaging has found that people with complicated grief have brain activity in areas that are known to be specifically linked with the longing for drugs and alcohol.[65] Sunshine children often face intense emotional pain and have few coping skills to manage it. This makes mind-altering substances seem appealing since they offer a way to get temporary relief from distress. However, this escape from mental pain comes at a high social and physical cost.

It is important that you talk with your sunshine child about substance use and the physical and emotional toll that it inevitably takes. Do not shy away from talking about the real risks, including death, that come with drug use. Talk frankly with your sunshine child about how substance use could prevent them from meeting their own goals. If you are concerned that they are already using substances, ask them about this directly.

If you discover that your child is already using drugs, it is important that you seek help immediately. Once sunshine children become addicted to any substance, it is incredibly difficult, if not impossible for them to stop using it on their own. Over time, their need for the substance can cause them to do things that they would never do if it were not for their addiction. They may steal, lie, or engage in illegal behaviors. Consequently, it can be very difficult to parent a child who is addicted to substances. It is important that you remind yourself that your sunshine child's addiction is an illness, not a choice, while refusing to enable their behavior.

Dealing with substance use and abuse can be frustrating and overwhelming for everyone involved. However, treatment is available. If your sunshine child is struggling with a substance use problem, staff at SAMHSA's National Helpline (1-800-662-4357) can connect you with confidential treatment options and important information about local resources. Alternatively, you can contact your insurer for a list of facilities that participate in your insurance plan. If you are uninsured, your state Agency for Substance Abuse Services can help to direct you to the appropriate programs and support groups. Finally, some general mental health providers may be willing and qualified to work with children who have substance use disorders.

Warning Signs

If you have ever called a doctor's office, chances are good that you heard an "If this is an emergency, please hang up and call 911" message. In other words, the office is communicating: "If your situation might be more than we can handle, change your plans and call for immediate help." There are times when parents of grieving children must make a similar change of plans. Even parents who have done everything right can find themselves caring for a sunshine child who is in crisis. If you reach this point, you need to get help as soon as possible.

One of the best ways to determine if your sunshine child is in danger is to talk with them. There was a time when mental health professionals thought that talking about things like suicide and substance use would make children more likely to engage in these behaviors. However, we now understand that the opposite is true. By talking about mental health struggles, parents give their children the opportunity to seek assistance that they need from the people who care about them the most. Children who talk with their parents about difficult topics are ultimately less likely to engage in dangerous behaviors and more likely to get help when they do.

Psychological Red Flags

- Your child says that they want to commit suicide (this is particularly concerning if they have been preparing or have a specific plan about how they might attempt it)

- Your child is threatening or attempting to harm themselves or others

- Your child is acting bizarrely or in ways that do not make sense

- Your child is experiencing hallucinations or delusions that are causing him or her to lose touch with reality

- Your child has overdosed or consumed something dangerous[66]

- Your child has attempted suicide[67]

A child who is showing signs of a psychological emergency should never be left alone. Ensure that your sunshine child cannot access anything that is potentially dangerous such as guns, knives, ropes, matches, sharp objects, and medications. If you can safely drive your child to the emergency room, do that. Otherwise, bring your child with you and watch them while you call the suicide hotline (988)[68] or emergency services (911). Then do whatever is needed to keep your child calm while waiting for help. Many children who are suicidal or psychotic are terrified, so it is important that you manage your own anxiety so that you can be as reassuring as possible.

It is possible that you may need assistance from police, EMTs, or a Mobile Crisis Unit that is trained in assessing and assisting with psychological emergencies. If this is the case, it is important that you make sure that any emergency responders know that your sunshine child is having a mental health crisis because this information may not have been conveyed to them by dispatchers and it is easy to misunderstand what is happening in tense situations. Also, try to keep your sunshine child calm and prevent them from doing anything that may be viewed as aggressive. Emergency service personnel are coming into a high stress situation and this can prime them to be on alert for perceived threats. Similarly, make sure that neither of you is holding anything that could be misconstrued as a weapon and alert them to any weapons you may have in your home. Most importantly, do your best to help your child to follow the responders' instructions. While it can be scary to have emergency services descend on your home, they are often the safest way to get your sunshine child the help that they need.

During a mental health emergency, the faster you get help, the better, so do not hesitate to act if you are concerned for your sunshine child. Once you have made the decision to seek help, avoid the temptation to second guess yourself. It can be easy to convince yourself that you are just overreacting because a large part of you wishes that this was the case. However, there is a reason that the saying, "it is always better to be safe than sorry" has become a cliché: it is true.

Checking In

I suspect that this section of the book was difficult to read. It is not easy to think about our children's profound suffering and you may be finishing this section of the book and thinking, "I thought she said the point of this book was to provide some hope that things don't have to be so bad. That was terrifying and depressing!"

While it may not have been easy reading, the knowledge that you have gained is going to be one of the biggest things that your sunshine child has going for them. Your sunshine child needs a parent who has a realistic understanding of what they are going through. They need a parent who can identify their behaviors as reflections of their emotions and who can take their hand and say, "I see you are hurting, lets walk together." They also need a parent who can manage their own emotions so that they can effectively navigate emergency situations. A parent who can do those things is one of the most effective antidotes against the ravages of grief that your child can have. By powering through this difficult material, you have prepared yourself to be exactly that kind of parent for your child.

In the final chapters, we will explore the ways that faith can impact grieving siblings and consider what happens when children grieve well. Even though you may feel heavy with the weight of what you have just read, remember that there is hope ahead.

Raising Sunshine

CHAPTER EIGHTEEN: FAITH IN THE FACE OF LOSS

"The most beautiful people we have known are those who have known defeat, known suffering, known struggle, known loss, and have found their way out of the depths...Beautiful people do not just happen."
- Dr. Elisabeth Kubler Ross

"Do not fear death. Death is always at our side. When we show fear, it jumps at us faster than light. But if we do not show fear, it casts its eye upon us gently and guides us into infinity."
-Laughing Bull

To be completely honest, I wrestled with whether to include this chapter in the book. I wanted my writing to be accessible to all grieving families and I know that, for some of us, religion and faith conjure up negative and hugely painful emotions. In fact, I have seen firsthand how infant death can cause thoughts about God - or any similar intelligent, omnipotent being[69] - to feel like a cosmic slap in the face. At the same time, though, I am certain that the only reason I survived my loss was my faith. Any hope that my words can offer pales in comparison to the strength, comfort, and hope that I received from my relationship with God. I could not imagine writing a book about helping children to survive the loss of an infant sibling if I omitted the most important part of my family's grief journey. As a result, I tentatively began researching how faith and religion impact families that have lost a child.

What I found through my investigation convinced me that I could not leave this chapter out of my book because I am not alone in finding hope in my religious beliefs.[70] In fact, because religion seeks to provide answers to the meaning of life and what comes after our time spent on this earth, many people discover that their faith is strengthened by their grief even as it is giving them the strength to persevere.

What Science Says About Religion and Grief [71]

In a study of bereaved siblings, many participants reported that their loss motivated them to seek answers to big questions about life, death, and God. Parents are also often driven to find meaning in their child's death and their own survival. In fact, Bakker and Paris wrote, "Parental bereavement is an especially intense and formative element of religious experience." One study found that over sixty two percent of parents actively sought out religious meaning when their child died![72]

It makes sense that death causes us to ask big questions about things that don't have easy answers. Infant death presents an existential crisis and challenges the assumptions that we may have previously held about our world. This forces us to reevaluate things that we once thought we understood or took for granted. Consequently, our religious beliefs often grow, change and strengthen as we grieve. Fyodor Dostoevsky picked up on this unique time in our spiritual lives when he wrote, "The darker the night, the brighter the stars, The deeper the grief, the closer is God!" In the days after Noemi's death, I truly felt as if somehow what had happened altered the veil between Heaven and Earth, making the one seem far less distant from the other.

As suggested previously, a major reason that religious beliefs can be so helpful to us is that they offer a way to make sense of our loss. Many mental health providers feel that meaning making is an important part of healthy grieving and studies have shown that grieving parents report less severe grief when they are able to find purpose in their loss.[73] As Dr. Richard Goldstein wrote, "Better grief outcomes rely on a parent's ability to find meaning in their child's life or death." So, the very act of asking the big questions can help people to navigate their journey through grief in healthy ways.

Of course, because there are so many different types and expressions of religious beliefs, the relationship between religion and infant loss is complicated. On the one hand, as we have discussed, there is good evidence that religious faith is very helpful to grieving families. In fact, a survey of the studies that examine this topic found that ninety-four percent suggest that adherence to religion has a positive impact on grief.[74] For example, one study of bereaved siblings found that Catholic children who lost a sibling were less likely to experience a decline in the number of school years they complete when compared to non-Catholic bereaved siblings.[75] [76] A different study found that parents who regularly attended religious services prior to their child's death experienced less anxiety and depression than parents who did not attend religious services regularly.[77] If you are still skeptical, consider these various study findings:

- ✓ People who identify themselves as having a strong faith experience less severe grief after a traumatic loss.[78] [79]

- ✓ Seventy three percent of women reported that their religious beliefs helped them to navigate their grief.[80]

- ✓ In one study, it was extremely important for Black women who lost a pregnancy to keep "developing, renewing, or retaining a relationship with God," even when they did not identify with a particular religious tradition.[81]

- ✓ Black women described finding comfort in the assurance that God has a reason for their loss, He can fix anything, and He is their protector.[82]

- ✓ Prayer provided grieving parents with strength and comfort. [83]

- ✓ Families felt that their religious beliefs helped them to grieve.[84]

- ✓ It was rare for grieving families to describe their baby as being gone or non-existent. Instead, most families maintained the hope that they would one day be reunited with their baby and their religious beliefs helped to shape their hopes and expectations for what that reunification might ultimately look like.[85]

✓ While beliefs about what happens after death vary significantly, almost all of them offer reassuring hope to grieving families.[86]

Research data make it clear that many families find great comfort in their religious beliefs; however, there is evidence that, at least initially, religion can be upsetting to some. For example, many teenage siblings report feeling anger at God for allowing their sibling's death.[87] Parents, too, often feel a palpable fury toward God for what has happened. They feel betrayed and unsure of their faith. Some even believe that their child's death is punishment from a vengeful God.

In one study, almost forty percent of parents reported that they experienced a crisis of faith after their child died.[88] One parent said that this untimely loss "ripped up my faith like a paper shredder." Another described an overwhelming and "deep sense of unknowing." Research suggests that parents and siblings who are unable to resolve their religious struggles are more likely to have a difficult time moving on after their loss.[89] These individuals also tend to experience grief that is very intense and long-lasting.

Another study found that when religion is a positive and integrated part of someone's life, it helps them to handle their grief. However, when a person's faith is challenged by uncertainty or rigid and inflexible, such beliefs tend to complicate the grieving process.[90] This sheds light onto why there are many conflicting findings in the research about religion and grief.

Religious Communities

The religious community that a person participates in also helps to determine whether religious beliefs are helpful or hurtful. Many grieving parents reported that their interactions with people in their religious communities were deeply wounding. They were often upset by platitudes such as "God doesn't give more than you can handle," or "God must have wanted another angel." Others were upset when those in their faith community had trouble accepting the pain and struggle that are inescapable experiences of the bereavement process. Certain religious traditions are better equipped to incorporate pain and suffering as an expected part of life. Those that struggle to make sense of pain can cause followers who are experiencing it to feel like they are doing something wrong. I was astounded when a well-meaning person suggested that, because of my faith, I should be thriving instead of merely surviving my child's death.

In addition to experiencing additional pain caused by interactions with members of their religious community, many grieving families feel too overwhelmed and worn out by their grief to participate in these communities. Their exhaustion can make social connections and vibrant worship feel impossible. People who are more introverted may also find it difficult to muster the courage and energy simply to be in public while they grieve. For such people, navigating a coffee and donut hour after a religious service feels like torture.

A community's focus on miracles can also be problematic for families mourning an infant. Some families reported that they were upset by stories about miracles and blessings because they wondered, "Why didn't I get a miracle?" or "Why didn't I deserve the blessing of a baby, too?"[91] These feelings are often exacerbated by the way that common interpretations of miracle stories tend to imply that God performed a miracle because of someone's faith or prayers. This understandably leaves grieving parents and siblings thinking, "Were my prayers not enough?" or "How could anyone have had more faith than I did, yet God didn't act!" These stories bring both our own level of faithfulness and God's justice into question. The reality is, that the death or survival of an infant is in no way due to merit.

Finally, many religious communities come together to celebrate the birth of a baby. Rituals like circumcision, dedication and baptism can be unbearably painful for parents whose baby will never participate in these events. As a result, many grieving families distance themselves from their religious communities when their child dies.

Returning to Faith

Despite the early challenges, most families that initially struggle with their faith, eventually return to their religious communities and traditions. Some find their negative reactions subside over time and others figure out ways to incorporate their sorrows into their religious beliefs. Many of these families return to their faith with new insights and practices. Their journeys back to faith can involve writing, meditating, spending time in nature and participating in religious rituals. Families build relationships with religious leaders who are able to listen to their experiences and to sensitively provide insight into how their faith can help them bear their pain. These families grow to see their faith as a source of strength, hope, and comfort,[92] even though they may have initially experienced distress.

Lasting Questions

Families that find religion to be helpful recognize that religion itself does not answer the question of why a baby dies. As time passes, many families eventually stop looking for an answer to "Why?" Instead, they come to accept that religious beliefs can offer them peace, comfort, hope and meaning, even if they never understand the "why." They learn to live with the tension between what they know to be true about their faith and what remains unknowable. In fact, if they are like me, they grow to love the mere act of releasing the need to know and abandoning themselves to what they believe.

Apart from the beliefs and traditions of various religious groups, religious communities themselves often serve as the primary supporters of grieving families. I witnessed this firsthand at my graduate school which attracted many students from a tightly knit Jewish community. During our time there, one of the students faced a serious pregnancy complication that had a huge impact on her family. The community mobilized and ensured that the student and her family received needed practical and emotional care. As an outsider looking in, this experience helped me to understand the depth of support and protection that a religious community can provide for families facing difficult circumstances.

Helping Your Sunshine Child to Access the Gift of Faith

Some of us were raised in families that were steeped in religious traditions. In such families, faith permeates daily life. Other families, however, are not used to thinking about religious ideas and beliefs. Some may even have had negative experiences that left them feeling alienated from their religious communities. Wherever you lie on this spectrum, there are some basic things you can do to help your sunshine child access the faith that you want to share with them so that they can benefit from it as they grieve.

1. **Regularly Attend Religious Meetings Together**

   Many religious groups meet at a predictable time to practice their traditions and learn about their faith. If you are curious about the possible benefit of religious beliefs, I encourage you to make a point of regularly attending religious meetings with your children. Studies show that when children and adolescents attend regular religious services, they tend to be happier as young adults. They are also less likely to abuse drugs and have lower rates of STDs than their peers who did not regularly participate in religious services during childhood.[93] This suggests that, regardless of the value that your own belief system places on such formalized ritual, the practice does benefit families in concrete ways.

   Attending religious meetings takes work and planning, especially at first. It can be difficult to get everyone up and moving for early morning services and it can be hard to carve out time for meetings that happen later in the day. Additionally, for families with young sunshine children, religious services can feel like one big wrestling match. Ever since my rainbow son was born, Sunday afternoon is always when my back is sorest! As a result, many parents are not able to get much out of religious meetings while their children are young, so they often stop going all together. All too often, those that try to attend are pushed away by unwelcoming individuals who are annoyed by the antics of their children.

My advice is to keep going anyway. The more your kids get used to attending these services, the more they will conform to the behavioral expectations you set for them. More importantly, they will recognize that this is something you value enough to do what it takes to be there – even when that includes tackling them repeatedly. Hopefully, your sunshine child will begin to take on your beliefs as an important part of their own lives and will become more engaged over time.

You might find the following to be helpful ideas to get you through the religious meetings that can seem never-ending to a young child and their parent:

- ✓ "Fidget" toys that don't make noise

- ✓ Snacks and drinks that are self-contained, spill-proof and not crunchy

- ✓ Noiseless toys, like an etch-a-sketch (of course any toy is not noiseless when it is dropped - and it will be dropped)

- ✓ Books, activity books or coloring books (extra points if they relate to your religious beliefs)

- ✓ Bribes and threats (I am usually against using bribery and threats to parent my children, but I admit that I have resorted to promising candy if my children are quiet for "just a few more minutes" and threatening to take away TV time if they are not)[94]

Another important way to help your child to get through the meeting is to talk with them about your expectations beforehand, as well as clarifying what they can expect. If you are not sure what to expect yourself, consider attending a meeting alone before bringing your sunshine child, or tell them that you will guide them through it as you go. You can also try to quietly explain what is happening during the service. Often, religious meetings can overwhelm children's senses and make them confused, so your whispered explanations can help them to make sense of what is happening and foster their curiosity and interest.

Finally, remember that how your children behave (or don't) is ultimately out of your hands. Even with the best intentions and preparations, young children are going to make mistakes in unfamiliar religious settings. Just this past weekend, my four-year-old son, who was told to let us know if he needed to leave the sanctuary to use the bathroom, leaned over to me during church and loudly whispered, "I can't fart in Church because the smell distracts people from Jesus, right mommy?" While my immediate response was embarrassment (and some amusement), the truth is that I am glad that my son had the opportunity to say something so inappropriate in our place of worship because it meant that he was present in a place where he could learn about God and participate in our religious community. While it would have been better if he had not seized the opportunity, his words revealed that he was growing an awareness of both the purpose of our time in church and consideration for the people around him.

2. **Belong to A Faith Community**

Once you have chosen a religious meeting or service, do what you can to get to know and support that community. Are there special classes for you or your children (bonus points if these take your kids off your hands during the meeting)? Is there a conference or camp that your family can attend together? Are there community meals or after-service social times? Does the community sponsor any events that you could participate in or are there ways that you could volunteer to serve your community? Is there another family you could invite for a playdate or a community leader that you could invite to dinner?

Active involvement in your religious community will build relationships with people who share your beliefs while helping to expand a support network for both your sunshine child and you. Your engagement will also demonstrate to your Sunshine that you are truly invested in your beliefs, not just a passive participant.

3. **Pray or Meditate Daily**

In addition to regular participation in religious meetings, daily prayers, and meditation benefit children. In fact, one study found that young adults who have prayed or meditated daily since childhood were sixteen percent happier than their peers.[95] Daily prayer time also has benefits for the whole family. For example, researchers Chelladurai, Dollahite and Marks found that families that prayed together every day share their needs, support one another, and experience a needed respite from the daily grind. Such prayer time helps to develop a sense of trust and belonging between family members, as well as a space to work through challenges and decisions.

Unfortunately, it can be difficult to remember to keep prayer and meditation a part of our busy days. Families that do manage this tend to accomplish it by connecting their prayers or meditations to specific parts of their daily routines. For example, they always pray before meals, at bedtime, or before leaving the house for the day. Sometimes, families pray specific prayers at certain times of the day, or after completing certain tasks or scheduled activities. We once had neighbors whose days were punctuated by this kind of ritualized prayer and their daughter knew that she could not come over after school until she had prayed at home. Another way that families incorporate prayer into their lives is by using traditional prayers to mark holidays or a special day of the week (like Shabbat or the Sabbath). By connecting prayers and meditation to activities, times, or events, they become habits that punctuate our lives and prayer becomes a comforting activity for our sunshine children.

4. **Use Your Home**

My husband and I enjoy watching crime shows after our children are asleep. It is an unfortunate habit that I sometimes regret when if find myself alone late at night. However, it always fascinates me to observe how detectives can enter an empty house and leave with so much knowledge about the people who live there. In many ways, our homes are a physical representation of our values and personalities. What we choose to keep or discard, the pictures that decorate our walls, and the equipment we use for activities all tell a part of the story about who we are, what we love, and what we believe. Likewise, how we furnish and decorate our homes teaches our children about our faith. In some Catholic circles, this idea is called the "theology of home" which literally means "the study of God through the home." In other words, our sunshine children learn about our faith through our homes and what we choose to keep or exclude from them.

While I do not recommend that you do a complete home make-over to make your home a better teacher of your faith, I do suggest that you think consciously about what you bring into your home. As you buy new things, consider prioritizing objects that communicate what you believe. Your possessions can be used to literally surround your sunshine child with the ideas and truths that you hold most dear to your heart. For example, we keep a favorite statue in our home that depicts a figure of Jesus tenderly cradling a tiny baby on his shoulder. For us, it is a visual reminder of our trust that Noemi is having every need cared for by a loving Father in Heaven. While we have never explicitly talked about the statue, its hopeful and comforting message is communicated to our Sunshine whenever she looks at it.

5. **Get to the Heart of Traditions**

Kids love and thrive on traditions. Many have religious roots, but sometimes these origins get lost in the festivities. However, traditional celebrations offer unique and special opportunities to share your religious beliefs with your sunshine children. One way to do this is to find children's books that offer easy-to-understand explanations about a tradition and its history. For example, on December 6th, our family celebrates Svaty Mikulas (St. Nicholas) Day because that is part of our Czech-Catholic tradition. While we participate in many cultural activities on that day, one of my children's favorite ways that we celebrate is reading stories about the real Svaty Mikulas and then watching the St. Nicholas Veggie Tales movie. These religious stories become the focus of our celebrations and help us to remember why we celebrate.

There are many ways to use crafts, recipes, and hands-on activities to center your family on the roots of various traditions. You can find idea books at your library, through your faith community, or online. Don't be afraid to start small and pick one age-appropriate way to incorporate your beliefs into your celebrations. You and your Sunshine will likely find that your traditions are richer and you will simultaneously be giving your sunshine new tools to access faith.

6. **Encourage Service and Activism**

Sometimes religious beliefs can feel sterile and inapplicable to the realities of our daily lives. It is almost as though our spiritual life never intersects with our physical life. This disconnect can make it difficult to access the benefits of our faith during our grief. One of the ways that we can breach this divide between the spiritual and the physical is by participating in service and activism that aligns with our beliefs. In effect, rather than just saying, "This is what I believe," we are claiming, "This is what I believe and this is the difference it makes in my life and my world." It makes faith ours in a way that is potent and tangible. The Bible puts it this way:

> *"What good is it, my brothers and sisters, if someone claims to have faith but has no deeds? Can such faith save them? Suppose a brother or a sister is without clothes and daily food. If one of you says to them, "Go in peace; keep warm and well fed," but does nothing about their physical needs, what good is it? In the same way, faith by itself if it is not accompanied by action, is dead. But someone will say, "You have faith; I have deeds." Show me your faith without deeds, and I will show you my faith by my deeds."*
>
> – James 2:14-18

While many sunshine children are too young to engage in service activities and activism on their own, you can find activities that you can do together. For example, peaceful protests and assemblies can offer sunshine children and their parents opportunities to work toward change that reflects their beliefs or values. Parents can also involve their Sunshines as they drop off donations, help fund-raise for a charity, or give an Angel Tree or Operation Shoe Box gift. For families whose finances are tight, volunteering, visiting a nursing home, helping an elderly neighbor, or picking up trash at a beach can also be great ways to put belief into action.

However you do it, acts of service and activism make our beliefs come alive with meaning and conviction. As a result, they help our sunshine children to incorporate faith into their own lives.

7. **Support Your Child's Efforts**

Just as children grow in their relationships with their parents and in their knowledge of the world, they grow in their religious beliefs over time. You can encourage your child to explore their developing faith in several ways:

- ✓ Be positive about their efforts to learn about and practice the various traditions of your faith.

- ✓ Encourage your children to think deeply for themselves, rather than feeding them automatic responses.

- ✓ Guide your children as they explore their faith rather than imposing yours on them.

- ✓ Provide them with what they need to grow their beliefs, whether books, journals, mentors, community, or time.

- ✓ Ask them questions about their beliefs and experience of religion.

- ✓ Allow your children to wrestle with big questions and let them know that it is okay not to have all the answers.

8. Help Your Sunshine Child to Differentiate Faith from Followers

One of the most difficult things for religious parents living in today's world is the reality that our religions and religious communities do (or have a history of doing) terrible things that contradict the very religious beliefs they hold. The reality is that no religion has ever been executed perfectly by all its believers. As a result, we are repeatedly forced to wrestle with our faith when trusted religious leaders fail, harm, and disappoint us. However, this does not mean that what we believe is not true. Rather, the failures of religious leaders and our fellow believers remind us that there is a Truth that is bigger and better than us and that this Truth is worth striving for.

It can be difficult for children (and parents) to tease apart this distinction between religious teachings and the actions of its followers, but it is an important understanding to develop. You can help your sunshine child by teaching them that we all do and will make mistakes, but that doesn't change the reality about what we should have done. Use examples from your own experiences to help your children understand this abstract concept. For example, if you lose your temper with your child, apologize and tell your child that you were not acting in a way that aligns with your beliefs about the kind of parent you should be. You can also use examples from history, television, and literature to show that sometimes deceitful people twist the truth, but that does not make it untrue (Ursula from the Little Mermaid, Prince Hans from Frozen, and Mother Gothel from Tangled offer useful examples for this lesson).

While it can be tempting to ignore the wrongs done in the name of religion, doing so only delays your sunshine child's inevitable encounter with hypocrisy and confusion, setting up the possibility that they will lose trust in you and the things that you have taught them. If you are open (in age-appropriate ways) about times when religious followers have failed to live the teachings of their religions, you can help your child to differentiate between religious truth and human error.

9. Teach by Example

Apart from seeking Divine assistance, the single most important thing a parent can do to help their sunshine child to access their religious tradition is to lead by example: in other words, practice what you preach. Whether we like it or not, our actions have a huge impact on our kids. This fact can feel overwhelming, but our ability to influence our children is a gift and a powerful tool. Dr. Tim Kimmel, in his book, *Why Christian Kids Rebel*, explains that kids hear their parents talking about life's most important questions and then watch carefully to see how they respond to real life issues. If children see that their parents' teaching is consistent with the way that they live, they are more likely to see their parent's faith as authentic and religion as important.

On the flip side, if kids see their parents living as though the answers to life's big questions are irrelevant or meaningless, the kids are likely to decide that their parents must not really believe the things that they say they do. Can we blame them if they decide not to believe it either?

If your religious beliefs are a priority for you, if you seek comfort from your faith as you grieve, and if you are at ease when you talk about your beliefs and participate in religious traditions, your child will begin to recognize the value of your religious traditions and seek to grow their own faith. If you acknowledge your mistakes and the times that you do not live in a way that reflects your beliefs, you help your Sunshine to differentiate between the failings of religious followers and the truth that transcends them. If you are honest with your sunshine child (and yourself) about your doubts and unanswered questions, they will trust truths that you are confident of, while learning to live with their own inevitable doubts.

In the Catholic Church, it is often said that "parents are the first teachers" when it comes to faith. This is true, but not because of any great sermons they preach or wordy lectures they give. Instead, we are our children's first teachers through the example of our lives. Watching us live our own faith journey is the primary way that children learn to trust, value and access religion, regardless of how messy and complicated that journey may be.[96]

Raising Sunshine

CHAPTER NINETEEN: HOPE THAT SUNSHINES WILL SHINE

"The harder the pain, the longer the path to recovery, the better the opportunity to learn."
- Maxim Legace

"The highest tribute to the dead is not grief but gratitude."
– Thornton Wilder

If you have made it to this point in the book, it is safe to say that you understand the challenges that your sunshine child will face because of their sibling's death. You also have a sense of how to help your family navigate these challenges together. What you need now is a final dose of hope that will help you to picture what overcoming grief might look like for your child.

At the beginning of the book, I shared my motivation for writing. I was unable to find hopeful, but realistic information to help me parent my Sunshine. This is unfortunate because when you dive into the research and you learn about well-known, successful people who have lost a sibling, you begin to realize that there is more to the story than risk factors, negative impacts, and trauma. In fact, seemingly against the odds, many grieving brothers and sisters grow to be adults who live fully and well, demonstrating remarkable strength – some of which was likely forged in their grief. History's examples of these survivors of sibling loss offer you a reason to hope as you parent your Sunshine.

Nevertheless, there can be no doubt that the life and death of your baby will impact your sunshine child. Bereaved siblings speak about their dead brothers and sisters long after the death. They cherish photos and other tangible reminders of their siblings' brief lives. In many ways, our Sunshines are living testaments to the reality that they are "once a brother or sister, always a brother or sister." In fact, when sunshine children acknowledge their loss, make sense of it, and incorporate it into their identity, they can deal with the trauma of sibling death in a healthy way. This allows them to seize the life that they have been given and to grow in ways that they would not have grown otherwise. In a sense, their grief allows them to become the unique and amazing individuals that they are growing up to be.

My own sunshine daughter understands her family as consisting of her parents, her two sisters (we experienced a twelve-week miscarriage of a little girl following Noemi's death) and her baby brother. My Sunshine's sisters remain a central part of who she understands herself to be.

Another unique aspect of sunshine children is the result of their being forced to grow-up quickly when a sibling dies. In our case, my Sunshine went from being a happy, naïve toddler to a realistic, sturdy, and mature young girl almost overnight. In many ways, who she was vanished with her sister's death as her development was accelerated by difficulty. This happened for several reasons. First, she was suddenly aware of the chasm between fairytale promises of "happily-ever-afters" and the unexpected – and sometimes unwanted – twists and turns of real life. However, when I am honest with myself, I know that part of her seemingly sudden maturity was her response to my need for her to be more independent and self-sufficient as I grieved. Now that time has passed, there are many times that she is "just a kid" but she is also wise beyond her years.

My Sunshine is not alone in this transformation. Bereaved siblings frequently report having to grow-up quickly. This can present challenges for them, but it can also be an asset if they build on their hard-earned maturity as they grow. Sunshines are uniquely prepared to seize opportunities that arise and to make choices that are based on knowledge and insight that their peers have yet to gain.

Let Me Introduce You to My Sunshine Child Six Years After Her Loss

Today, my sunshine daughter is passionate, vibrant, and strong with an intense and contagious love of life. She has weathered storms that would have challenged my coping abilities at her age, and she has done so with incredible grace and kindness. My daughter is acutely aware of injustice in her world and has been unafraid to fight for justice, even when it costs her to do so. She is a loyal and beloved friend who is quick to forgive and unbelievably social. She is a wonderful big sister who treasures her little brother even during their most difficult interactions because she knows that his existence was not a given. Traditional ideas of a "well-behaved woman" or "elegant princess" do not limit her: she is becoming a woman in the fullest sense of the word. She is a deep thinker and her questions often challenge me and her father to think about things in new and deeper ways. Her love of nature has profoundly changed the way I see the world and opened me up to the world of Native Gardening, which has become one of my own great pleasures. Her affection for the natural world she lives in has driven her to educate many about the dangers facing it and her passion has pushed children and adults in our community to be better stewards of the local environment. She is not perfect and she has her struggles, but she makes my life better and she makes me a better person, too. I have no doubt that she will continue to leave her mark on the world in wonderful ways.

Additionally, because bereaved siblings have had to face and wrestle with reality at an early age, they often learn effective coping strategies while they are still living in home environments that provide them with safe, nurturing spaces to practice. They are then able to use these skills when they face future problems and adversity. Weathering grief builds resilience and grit in our Sunshines. This resiliency is strengthened by the fact that many of them have developed deep and lasting relationships with their caregivers through their shared grief journey. These bonds offer them support throughout their lives.

Although research about the positive outcomes associated with sibling death is scarce, it does exist. One such study found that bereaved siblings who have a dedicated support network tend to be more future-oriented than their peers.[97] This is not surprising since bereaved siblings frequently say that their loss helped them to value life more due to their acute awareness that tomorrow is not promised. Unlike their peers who often do not begin to think about their own mortality until much later in life, sunshine children know that their life is finite and they often exhibit an eagerness to take advantage of the time that they have. Their loss seems to motivate them to define and achieve goals. Counterintuitively, studies show that sunshine children tend to have a more positive outlook than their peers.[98]

Another small study of surviving siblings documents that sunshine children tend to make goals that are "worthwhile" and more consistently act in moral ways.[99] Somehow, the experience of sibling death seems to clarify and the sunshine children's value systems. Perhaps this is because their loss has forced them to contemplate big questions including, but not limited to, the meaning of life and death. It makes sense that thinking about such big philosophical ideas would help Sunshines to develop a strong sense of morality.

Finally, bereaved siblings have reported that their experience of loss helped them to become more compassionate, caring, and empathic people.[100] As is often the case, experiencing their own pain sensitizes sunshine children to the suffering of others. They become more attuned to the struggles of others and are better able to imagine what other people might be feeling. Additionally, many sunshine children report that their loss has helped them to become better listeners.[101] This is perhaps because this skill was modelled for them by the adults who helped them to navigate grief.

Mature

Resilient

Goal-oriented

Moral

Compassionate

Empathic

Most parents would be thrilled and thankful to have their children described in such terms. In fact, these are the very traits that researchers have identified in sunshine children! It is easy to see these qualities in the life stories of many famous people who lost their siblings. Marie Curie's relentless pursuit of knowledge, President Lincoln's honesty, and Coretta Scott King's activism all depend on these traits that are associated with bereaved children. Reflection on this raises some interesting questions:

- ✓ Would Eleanor Roosevelt have been so concerned about the welfare of women if she had not experienced her own painful losses?

- ✓ Would St. Therese of Lisieux have been so focused on the importance of little everyday actions if her losses had not taught her what a gift is contained in each moment?

- ✓ If his childhood had not been full of adversity, would Martin Luther have developed such strong convictions that he was willing to give up everything to right the wrongs that he found in the Catholic Church?

Perhaps these individuals would have followed similar paths without their early experiences of loss and grief. However, the fact remains that sibling loss played a role in shaping each of these famous people into the legends we know them to be.[102]

As I raise my Sunshine, there are times when I feel discouraged. There are days when I feel overwhelmed by worry about the risks to her continued healthy development because of her sister's death. There are moments when I wonder if she has been damaged by the grief that she has experienced or by the ways that I have grieved. However, when I look at the strong young woman she is becoming, the deep and meaningful relationships that she is building, and the positive ways that her loss has shaped her passion and compassion, I cannot help but be hopeful for her.

Yes, sibling death is hard. But, like a diamond that can only be formed under tremendous pressure I have found that sometimes the most precious pieces of who we are form in the hardest times. That is why, if this book leaves you with nothing else, my hope is that it leaves you with the confidence that your Sunshine can shine.

Raising Sunshine

Raising Sunshine

BIBLIOGRAPHY

ABC News (2018). *Remembering Robin Bush, George H W Bush's daughter who died of leukemia in 1953.* 6abc.com/robin-bush-death-george-daughter-children/4808659

Academic Kids (n.d.). *Marlon Jackson.* http://academickids.com/encyclopedia/index.php/-Marlon_Jackson

Access Community Health Network (2019). *What are the warning signs of postpartum depression.* https://www.achn.net/about-access/whats-new/health-resources/what-are-the-warning-signs-of-postpartum-depression/

Acevedo, B.P., Aron, A., Fisher, H.E., & Brown, L.L. (2012). Neural correlates of long-term intense romantic love." *Social Cognitive and Affective Neuroscience, 7*(2), 145-159.

American Families of Faith Project (n.d.), https://americanfamiliesoffaith.byu.edu/family-processes-and-religion

American Psychiatric Association (2013). *Diagnostic and statistical manual of mental disorders (5th ed.) Addition.* Arlington, VA. https://doi.org/ib.1176/appi.books.9780890425596

American Psychiatric Association Division 12 (Society of Clinical Psychology) (2017). *How do I choose between medication and therapy.* https://www.apa.org/ptsd-guideline/patients-and-families/medication-or-therapy#:~:text=For%20anxiety%20disorders%2C%20cognitive%2Dbehavioral,improve%20outcomes%20from%20psychotherapy%20alone

Anderson, A. (n.d.). *Elizabeth Ann Seton.* womenshistory.org/education-resources/-biographies/elizabeth-ann-seton

Antenatal Results & Choices (n.d.). Help for same sex partners. https://www.arcuk.org/-publication/help-for-same-sex-partners

Anthony, C. (2013). *The children of Jaqueline Kennedy.* http://www.firstladies.org/blog/the-children-of-jacqueline-kennedy

Bado, K. (2018). *Touching cartoon reunites George H.W. Bush with wife Barbara and daughter Robin.* usatoday.com/story/news/politics-/2018/12/01/george-h-w-bush-reunited-barbara-and-robin-touching-cartoon/2172695002

Bakker, J.K. & Paris, J (2013). Bereavement and religion online: Stillbirth, neonatal loss, and parental religiosity. *Journal for the Scientific Study of Religion, 32*(1), 657-674.

Balk, D (1983). How teenagers cope with sibling death: Some implications for school counselors. *The School Counselor, 31*(2), 150-158.

Barthell, J. (2014). *American saint - The life of Elizabeth Seton.* New York: St. Martin's Press.

Baudouin-Croix, M. (1993). *Leonie Martin - A difficult life.* San Francisco: Ignatius Press.

Bauer, N. (2021). *Childhood adversity: Buffering stress and building resilience.* https://www.healthy-children.org/English/healthy-living/emotional-wellness/Building-Resilience/Pages/ACEs-Adverse-Childhood-Experiences.aspx

Bellefonds, C. & Greenberg, J. (2022). *Your first period after pregnancy loss.* https://www.whatto-expect.com/pregnancy/pregnancy-loss/first-period-after-miscarriage/

Bereavement and Loss Looking Onwards (2017). Separation anxiety after bereavement - Helping bereaved children and young people cope. *Balloons,* https://www.balloonscharity.co.uk/-wp-content/-uploads/2018/08/balloons-information-sheet-16.pdf

Bettelheim, B. (1987). *A good enough parent* (1st ed.). New York: Random House.

Billiar, C. (n.d.). *Lactation after infant loss.* n.d. https://icea.org/lactation-after-infant-loss/

Biswas-Diener, R. & Kashdan, T. (2014). *The right way to get angry.* https://greatergood.-berkeley.edu/article/item/the_right_way_to_-get_angry#:~:text=Anger%20is%20best%20viewed%20as,life%20or%20on%20the%20job.

Black History (n.d.). *10 things most people don't know about Coretta Scott King.* https://www.black-history.com/2018/07/coretta-scott-10-things-most-people-dont-know.html

Bluebond-Langner, M. (1980) *The private worlds of dying children.* Princeton: Princeton University Press.

Boyle, N. (2021). *Johann Wolfgang von Goethe.* https://www.britannica.com/biography/Johann-Wolfgang-von-Goethe>.

Burke, C.L. & Copenhaver, J.G. (2004) Animals as people in children's literature. *Language Arts,* 81(3) https://cdn.ncte.org/nctefiles/store-/samplefiles/journals/la/la0813animals.pdf

Burstein, M., Ginsburg, G., Tein, J. (2012). Parental anxiety and child symptomatology: An examination of additive and interactive effects of parent psychopathology." *Journal of Abnormal Child Psychology,* 897-909.

Busch, T. & Kimble, C.S. (2001). Grieving children: Are we meeting the challenge?" *Journal of Pediatric Nursing,* 27(4), 414-418.

Cabrera, F. & Stevenson, R. (2017). Dealing with loss and grief of minority children in an urban setting [Chapter 13]. *Children, adolescents and death - Questions and answers.* New York: Routledge.

Caroll, K., Noble-Carr, D., Sweeney, L., & Waldby, C. (2020). The 'lactation after infant death (AID) framework': A guide for online health information provision about lactation after stillbirth and infant death. *Journal of Human Lactation,* 36(3), 480-491.

Center For Disease Control and Prevention (CDC) (2021). *Risk and protective factors.* https://www.cdc.gov/violenceprevention/aces/risk-protectivefactors.html

Center For Substance Abuse Treatment (US). (2014). Understanding the impact of trauma. *Trauma informed care in behavioral health services.* Rockville, MD: Substance Abuse And Mental Health Services Administration (US). 10-11. https://www.ncbi.nlm.-nih.gov/books/NBK207191/-?report=reader#_NBK207191_pubdet_

Chaiyachati, B. (2020). *Children in foster care 42% more likely to die than children in the general population.* https://www.healio.com/news/-pediatrics/20200424/children-in-foster-care-42-more-likely-to-die-than-children-in-general-population

Chalmers, A. (2007). When siblings die, seeing the body may help. *Nursing Standard,* 22(4), 6-6.

Chansky, T. (2019). *Freeing your child from negative thinking - From toddlers to teens.* New York: Hachette Book Group.

Chelladurai, J., Dollahite, D. & Marks, L. (2018). The family that prays together: Relational process associated with family prayer. *Journal of Family Psychology,* 32(7), 849-859.

Christ, G.H., Bonanno, G., Malkinson, R., & Rubin, S. (2003). Appendix E: Bereavement experiences after the death of a child. *When children die: Improving palliative and end of life care for children and their families.* NY: National Academies Press. 553-579.

Christiansen, S, Reneflot, A., Stene-Larson, K., Hauge, L.J. (2020). Alcohol related mortality following the loss of a child: A register-based follow-up study from norway. *BMJ Open,* 10, 1-9.

Cleveland Clinic (2022) *EMDR therapy.* https://my.clevelandclinic.org/-health/treatments/22641-emdr-therapy

— Cleveland Clinic (2020). *Pain control after surgery.* https://my.clevelandclinic.org/health/-articles/11307-pain-control-after-surgery

— Cleveland Clinic (2018). *Pregnancy: Physical changes after delivery.* https://my.cleveland-clinic.org/health/articles/9682-pregnancy-physical-changes-after-delivery#:~:text=Lochia-%20is%20the%20vaginal%20-discharge,than%20a%20plum%2-C%20are%20normal

Cooney, B. (1996). *Eleanor.* New York, NY: Puffin Books.

Corinthios, A. (2015). *Stephen Colbert on learning to accept the deaths of his father and brothers: "I love the thing that I most wish had not happened".* people.com/tv/steven-colbert-plane-crash-killed-his-father-and-brothers-when-he-was-10/

Cowchock, F.S., Ellestad, S.E., Meador, K.G., Koenig, H.G., Hooten, E.G., Swamy, G.K. (2011). Religiosity is an important part of coping with grief in pregnancy after a traumatic second trimester loss. *Journal of Religion and Health,* 50(4), 901-910.

Craven, C. (n.d.). *About.* www.lgbtqreproductiveloss.org

— Craven, C. (2019). *Reproductive losses - Challenges to LGBTQ family-making.* New York: Routledge.

Donelly, K.F. (1988). *Recovering from the loss of a sibling.* New York: Dodd, Mead & Company.

Dreher, D. (2019). *Why talking about our problems makes us feel better.* https://www.psychology-today.com/us/blog/your personal-renaissance/201906/why-talking-about-our-problems-makes-us-feel-better

Dundy, E. (2004). *Elvis and Gladys.* Jackson: University Press of Mississippi.

Dunne, R. (2021). *How to redeem loss in blended families.* hardinlife.com/-blog/2021/11/15/how-to-redeem-loss-in-blended-families

Dyregrov, A., Matthiesen, S. (1987). Anxiety and vulnerability in parents following the death of an infant. *Scandinavian Journal of Psychology,* 16-25.

Earl, J. (2017). *19 Celebrities you didn't know were twins.* https://www.cbs-news.com/pictures/-celebrities-you-didnt-know-were-twins/20/

Editorial Staff at American Addiction Centers. (2022). *The link between grief and addiction.* https://americanaddictioncenters.org/link-between-grief-and-addiction

EdSullivan.com. (n.d.). *About Ed Sullivan.* https://www.edsullivan.com/-about-ed-sullivan/

Encyclopedia of World Biography. (n.d.). *Diego Rivera biography.* https://www.notable-biographies.com/Pu-Ro/Rivera-Diego.html-#ixzz12GO9KaN6His

Evans, M. (2020). The relentlessness of black grief. *The Atlantic,* https://www.theatlantic.com/-ideas/archive/2020/09/relentless-ness-black-grief/616511/

Field, T. (2018). Why physical touch matters for your well-being. *Greater Good Magazine,* https://greatergood.berkeley.edu/article/-item/why_physical_touch_matters_for_your_well_being

Fisher, L. M. (2012). *Saint Kateri Tekakwitha - Courageous faith.* St. Paul: Pauline Books & Media.

Fletcher, J., Mailick, M., Song, J., Wolfe, B. (2013). A sibling death in the family: Common and consequential. *Demography, 50*(3), 203-826.

Fornari, M. & Schott, M. (2020). *What to do when your child has a mental health emergency.* riseandshine.childrensnational.org/what-to-do-when-your-child-has-a-mental-health-emergency/

Funk, A.M., Sheryl, J., Astroth, K. S., Braswell, G. (2018). A narrative analysis of sibling grief. *Journal of Loss & Trauma, 23*(1), 1-14.

Gallagher, T. (2021). A sister of St. Therese: Servant of God, Leonie Martin - bearer of hope. *Discerning Hearts Podcast,* (podcast episode 10). discerninghearts.com/catholic-podcasts/ep-10-a-sister-of-st-therese-servant-of-god-leonie-martin-bearer-of-hope-w-fr-timothy-gallagher-discerning-hearts-podcast/

Garcia, M. (2017). *The most beautiful - My life with Prince.* New York, NY: Hachette Books.

— Garcia, M. (2017). *Prince's ex-wife pens "love letter to his legacy".* https://www.hollywood-reporter.com/news/music-news/princes-wife-pens-love-letter-his-legacy-998602/

Gielen, N., Havermans, R., Tekelenburg, M. & Jansen, A. (2012). Prevalence of post-traumatic stress disorder among patients with substance use disorder: It is higher than clinicians think it is. *European Journal of Psychotraumatology, 3,* https://www.ncbi.-nlm.nih.gov/pmc/-articles/PMC3415609/

Goldstein, R.D. (2018). Parental grief. *SIDS sudden infant and early childhood death: The past, the present and the future.* Adelaide (AU): University of Adelaide Press. 143-154.

Government of Canada Department of Justice (2004). *High conflict separation and divorce: Options for consideration.* justice.gc.ca/-eng/rp-pr/fl-lf/divorce/2004_1/p3.html

Gray, P. (2015). *The good enough parent is the best parent.* https://www.psychologytoday.com/-us/-blog/freedom-learn/-201512/the-good-enough-parent-is-the-best-parent

Hadiah (2022). *Top 14 CBT exercises for anger management.* https://ineffableliving.-com/manage-your-anger/

Hammack, S., Cooper, M. & Lezak, K. (2012). Overlapping neurobiology of learned helplessness and conditioned defeat: Implications for PTSD and mood disorders. *Neuropharmacology, 62,* 565-575.

Harvard.edu (2018). *Religious upbringing linked to better health and well-being during early adulthood.* https://www.hsph.harvard.edu/-news/press-releases/religious-upbringing-adult-health/#:~:text=-Those%20who%20prayed%20or%20meditated,-who%20never%20-prayed%20or%20meditated.

Herberman, H.B., Fullerton, C.S., Ursano, R.J. (2013). Complicated grief and bereavement in young adults following close friend and sibling loss. *Depression and Anxiety, 30,* 1202-1210.

Holocaust Historical Society (n.d.). *Sigmund Freud and his sisters.* https://www.holocausthistorical-society.org.uk/contents/jewish-biographies/sigmund-freudandhissisters.html

Holohan, M. (2018). It is OK to feel it: One dad's mission to help men cope with pregnancy loss. *Today.* https://www.today.com/video/one-dad-s-mission-to-help-men-cope-with-pregnancy-loss-1368691779998

Houck, A.M. & Smentkowski, B.P. (2022). *Ruth Bader Ginsburg United States jurist.* https://www.britannica.com/biography/Ruth-Bader-Ginsburg

Isinger, C. & Stewart, H. (2021). What to do when you're drowning with Sally Clarkson. *Fountains of Carrots.* https://fountainsofcarrots.com/foc-162-what-to-do-when-youre-drowning-with-sally-clarkson/

Ivey, A.E., D'Andrea, M.J. & Ivey, M.B. (2011). *Theories of counseling and psychotherapy: A multicultural perspective.* Thousand Oaks: SAGE.

Jacobsen, H.K. (n.d.). *Martin Luther's early years: Did you know?* https://www.christianity-today.com/-history/issues/issue-34/-martin-luthers-early-years-did-you-know.html

Jaggi, M. (2001). *Ghosts at my shoulder.* https://www.theguardian.com/books/2001/mar/03/-fiction.features

Jang, C. & Lee, H. (2022). A review of racial disparities in infant mortality in the US." *Children (Basel),* 9(2), 257.

Karnaze, M.M. & Levine, L. (2018). Sadness, the architect of cognitive change." *The Function of Emotions.* 45-58.

Kassinove, H. (2012). *How to recognize and deal with anger.* https://www.apa.org/-topics/anger/-recognize

Kauros, C., Merrilees, C. & Cummings, E. (2008). Marital conflict and children's emotional security in the context of parental depression. *Journal of Marriage and Family,* 70(3), 684-697.

Keyes, K.M., Pratt, C., Galea, S., McLaughlin, K.A., Koenen, K.C., & Shear, M.K. (2014). The burden of loss: Unexplained death of a loved one and psychiatric disorders across the life course in a national study. *The American Journal of Psychiatry,* 171(8), 864-871.

Krell, R. & Rabkin, L. (1979). The effect of sibling death on the surviving child: A family perspective." *Family Process,* 8(4), 471-477.

Krisch, J. (2022). *What the loss of a child does to parents, psychologically and biologically.* https://www.fatherly.com/health-science/how-parents-experience-the-death-of-a-child/

Lamela, D. & Figuiredo, B. (2016). Coparenting after marital dissolution and children's mental health: A systematic review." *Jornal de Pediatricy,* 92(4), 331-342.

Larsen, N.E., Lee, K., & Ganea, P.A. (2018). Do storybooks with anthropomorphized animal characters promote prosocial behaviors in young children. *Developmental Science,* 21(3).

Levesque, J. (n.d.) *Finding support as an LGBTQ parent after the death of a child.* Itsconceivable-now.com/finding-support-as-an-lgbtq-parent-after-the-death-of-a-child

Levingston, S. (2013). *The Kennedy baby - The loss that transformed JFK.* NY: Diversion Books.

Library of Congress (2018). *Library of Congress Research Guides.* https://guides.loc.gov/navajo-code-talkers/profiles/john-kinsel

Lomas, T. (n.d.) The quiet virtues of sadness: A selective theoretical and interpretive appreciation of its potential contribution to wellbeing. *New Ideas in Psychology, 49,* 18-26.

Lullabytrust.org (n.d.) *If someone else's child dies in your care.* n.d. Website. 4 January 2023. https://www.lullabytrust.org.uk/bereavement-support/if-a-baby-dies-in-your-care/

MacDonald (2018) Transgender parents and chest/breastfeeding. https://kellymom.com/bf/got-milk/transgender-parents-chestbreast-feeding/#:~:text=Transgender%20men%20and%20women-%2C%20and,or%20have%20never%20given%20birth

March of Dimes.org https://www.marchofdimes.org/find-support/blog/-health-disparities-contribute-to-pregnancy-and-infant-loss

Mayo Clinic Staff. (2021). *Chronic stress puts your health at risk.* https://www.mayoclinic.org-/healthy-lifestyle/stress-management/-in-depth/stress/art-20046037

McNess, A. (2007). The social consequences of "how the sibling died" for bereaved young adults. *Youth Studies Australia, 26*(4).

McPhee, E. (2022). *Guilt in Remission – Workbook – Untreated guilt can grow in your body like cancer.* Independently published.

Melson, G.F. (2005). *Why the wild things are - Animals in the lives of children.* Cambridge, MA: Harvard University Press, 2005.

Metaxas, E. (2010). *Bonhoeffer - Pastor, martyr, prophet, spy.* Nashville, TN: Thomas Nelson, Inc,.

Michaelides, A. & Zis, P. (2019). Depression, anxiety and acute pain: Links and management challenges. *Postgraduate Medicine, 131*(7), 438-444.

Miller, A. (2013). Can this marriage be saved?. *Science Watch, 42.*

Miller, K. (2018). *Thriving with ADHD workbook for kids: 60 fun activities to help children self-regulate, focus, and succeed.* San Antonio: Althea Press.

Miscarriage Association (2022). Partners too. https://www.miscarriage-association.org.uk/-leaflet/-partners-too/

Mongin, H. (2015). *The extraordinary parents of St. Therese of Lisieux.* Huntington: Our Sunday Visitor, Inc,.

Moses-Kolko, E.L., Price, J.C., Wisner, K.L., Hanusa, B.H., Meltzer, C.C., Berga, S.L., Grace, A.A., di Scalea, T.L., Kaye, W.H., Becker, C. & Drevets, W.C. (2012). Postpartum and depression status are associated with lower [11C]raclopride BPnd in reproductive-age women. *Neuropsychopharmacology, 37,* 1422-1432.

Najman, J.M., Vance, J.C., Boyle, F., Embleton, G., Foster, B., & Thearle, J. (1993). The impact of a child death on marital adjustment. *Social Science & Medicine, 37*(8), 1005-1010.

National Park Service (2015). Abraham Lincoln autobiography. nps.gov/-abli/learn/news/-abraham-lincoln-autobiography.htm

—National Park Service (2021). "Thomas Lincoln Junior." nps.gov/abli/-learn/history-culture/-thomas-lincoln-junior.htm

New South Wales Ministry of Health (2018). *Breast care when your baby has died*. https://www.health.-nsw.gov.au/kidsfamilies/MCFhealth/-maternity/pages/breast-care-when-baby-has-died.aspx

NIDA (2020). *Drug misuse and addiction*. https://nida.nih.gov/-publications/drugs-brains-behavior-science-addiction/drug-misuse-addiction

Norton, R.J. (1996) Abraham Lincoln's Brother, Tommy Lincoln. *Abraham Lincoln Research Site*. rogerjnorton.com/Licoln93.html

Parlakian, R. (2019). *Coparenting tips when you're no longer together*. zerotothree.org/-resources/2879-coparenting-tips-when-you-re-no-longer-together

Phelps, H. (2015). *A profile of Carl Anderson part I: A Broadway legend with Lynchburg roots*. lynchburgmuseum.org/blog/2015/5/12/a-profile-of-carl-anderson-part-i-a-broadway-legend-with-lynchburg-roots

Pope Francis (2013, November 27). *Those who practice mercy do not fear death*. [General audience address]. Vatican. https://www.lastam-pa.it/vatican-insider/en/2013/11/27/-news/those-who-practice-mercy-do-not-fear-death-1.35961266

Pregnancy Birth and Baby (2019). *Fathers and miscarriage*. https://www.pregnancybirth-baby.org.au/-fathers-and-miscarriage

Price, J. (n.d.). *U.S. Department of Veteran Affairs - PTSD: National Center for PTSD*. https://www.ptsd.va.gov/professional/treat/specific/-parent_ptsd.asp

Rahman, I. (2022). *CBT for anger: How it works, techniques, & effectiveness*. https://www.choosing-therapy.com/cbt-for-anger/

Reach Out And Read (n.d.). *Reach out and read*. https://reachoutand-read.org/why-we-matter/child-development/

Reece, T. (2021). *Postpartum period: When will your menstrual cycle return after birth?* https://www.parents.com/pregnancy/my-body/-postpartum/your-period-after-pregnancy-what-to-expect/

Rosen, H. (1987). *Unspoken grief - Coping with childhood sibling loss*. Lexington, MA: Lexington Books.

Sabey, C., Charlton, C., & Charlton, S. (2018). The "magic" positive to negative interaction ratio. *Journal of Emotional and Behavioral Disorders*, 27(3), 154-164.

Saint John Paul II National Shrine (n.d.). *About Saint John Paul II*. https://www.jp2shrine.org/-en/about/jp2bio.html

Sands Stillbirth and Neonatal Death Charity (2014). Sexual relations after the death of a baby. https://www.sands.org.uk/sites/default/-files/AW%20Sexual%20realtionships%20SS%20LR%20WEB%202014.pdf

Sarkar, D. (2021). 5 things you didn't know about Marie Curie. *Discover Magazine*. https://www.discovermagazine.com/the-sciences/5-things-you-didnt-know-about-marie-curie

Sharpe, B. (2019). LGBTQ pregnancy loss and miscarriage often means grieving in the gaps. *Huffpost.com*. https://www.huffpost.com/-archive/ca/entry/lgbtq-miscarriage-support_ca_5da5cadde4b0058374e94b01

Sheehan, B. (2021). *Partners: Coping with loss*. https://www.baby-centre.co.uk/a1014770/-partners-coping-with-loss

Slater, M. (2015). *Dietrich Bonhoeffer and the death of Walter*. http://blog.bakeracademic.com/-dietrich-bonhoeffer-and-the-death-of-walter/

State Government Victoria Department of Education and Early Childhood Development & The University of Melbourne (2012). Reading to young children: A head start in life. *Victoria State Government Education and Training*. https://www.education.vic.gov.au/-documents/-about/research/readtoyoungchild.pdf

Substance Abuse and Mental Health Services Administration (n.d.). *SAMHSA's National Help Line*. https://www.samhsa.gov/find-help/national-helpline

Sudarsanan, S., Chaudhury, S., Pawar, A.A., Salujha, S.K. & Srivastava, K. (2004). Psychiatric emergencies. *Medical Journal of Armed Forces India*, 59-62.

Swanson, W.S. (2021). *How to ease your child's separation anxiety*. https://www.healthy-children.org/-English/ages-stages/toddler/-Pages/Soothing-Your-Childs-Separation-Anxiety.aspx

The Compassionate Friends (2020). Death of our stepchild or our partner's child. https://www.tcf.org.-uk/resources/L24-The-Death-of-a-Step-Child-C11R1707.pdf

—The Compassionate Friends (2021). Grieving child loss in blended and stepfamilies. https://www.tcf.org.uk/resources/Blended-and-StepFamilies-WEBVER1.0.pdf

—The Compassionate Friends (2020). The bereaved lone parent. https://www.tcf.org.uk/-resources/L17-The-Bereaved-Single-Parent-C07R1307.pdf

The Corrie Ten Boom House (n.d.). *The history of the ten Boom family*. www.corrietenboom.-com/en/family-ten-boom

The Legacy of Leo (2018). LGBT baby loss: A mission of mine. https://the-legacyofleo.com/-2018/02/22/lgbt-baby-loss-a-mission-of-mine/

The Mark Twain House and Museum. (2017). *Clemens family tree*. https://web.archive.-org/web/20170210081912/http://-www.marktwainhouse.org/man/clemens_family_tree.php

The Miscarriage Association (2016). Information sheet: LGBT pregnancy loss. Australian Psychological Society. https://psychology.org.au/-getmedia/9ea8dd55-7c2b-4653-8371-b1f732b70-b58/lgbt_-pregnancy_loss.pdf

The National World War II Museum New Orleans (n.d.). *The national World War II Museum New Orleans*. nationalww2museum.org

The Nobel Prize (n.d.). *Marie Curie* https://www.nobelprize.org/womenwhochangedscience/-stories/-marie-curie

Tommy's.org (2016). Dads feel the heartbreak of miscarriage too. https://www.tommys.org/about-us/charity-news/dads-feel-heartbreak-miscarriage-too

—Tommy's.org (n.d.). *Grieving for your baby after a stillbirth*. https://www.tommys.org/baby-loss-support/stillbirth-information-and-support/coping-grief-after-loss-baby-parents

Trifu, S., Vladuti, A. & Pompescu, A. (2019). The neuroendocrinological aspects of pregnancy and postpartum depression. *Acta Endocrinol,*

15(3), 410-415.

Unexpected Death of a Loved One Linked to Psychiatric Disorders. https://www.publichealth.-columbia.edu/public-health-now/news/unexpected-death-loved-one-linked-psychiatric-disorders

Ustundag-Budak, A.M., Larkin, M., Harris, G., & Blissett, J. (2015). Mothers' accounts of their stillbirth experiences and of their subsequent relationships with their living infant: An interpretive phenomenological analysis. *BMC Pregnancy and Childbirth,* 15, 263.

Van, P., & Meleis, A.I. (2003). Coping with grief after involuntary pregnancy loss: Perspectives on African American women. *Journal of Obstetric, Gynecological & Neonatal Nursing,* 32(1), 28-39.

Vance, J., Najman, J., Thearle, J., Embelton, G., Foster, W., Boyle, F. (1995). Psychological changes in parents eight months after the loss of an infant from stillbirth, neonatal death, or sudden infant death syndrome -- A longitudinal study. *Pediatrics,* 96, 933-938.

Volpicelli, J, Balaraman, G., Hahn, J., Wallace, H. & Bux, D. (1999). The role of uncontrollable trauma in the development of PTSD and alcohol addiction. *Alcohol Research and Health,* 23(4), 256-262.

Weiss, R. (1994). Drug will no longer be sold to stop breast milk. *Washington Post,* https://www.washingtonpost.com/-archive/lifestyle/wellness/1994/08/23/drug-will-no-longer-be-sold-to-stop-breast-milk/d991302a-5602-450e-87b0-97e049722579/

Wellborn, J. (2012). The experience of expressing and donating breastmilk following a perinatal loss. *Journal of Human Lactation,* 28(4), 506-510.

Women's Health.com Staff (2018). *Returning to work while grieving a miscarriage.* https://www.womenshealth.com.au/returning-to-work-miscarriage-grief/?category=-Erica_M_McAfee

Whiteman, S., McHale, S. & Soli, A. (2011). Theoretical perspectives on sibling relationships. *Journal of Family Theory and Review,* 3(2), 124-139.

Wilcox, W. & Dew, J. (2012). The date night opportunity - What does couple time tell us about the potential value of date nights. *The National Marriage Project.org.*

Winerman, L. (2005). Helping men to help themselves. *Monitor,* 36(7), 57.

Zero to three.org (2016). *Managing your own emotions: The key to positive, effective parenting.* https://www.zerotothrcc.org/-resource/managing-your-own-emotions-the-key-to-positive-effective-parenting/

Zisook, S. & Shear, K. (2009). Grief and bereavement: What psychiatrists need to know. *World Psychiatry,* 8(2), 67-74.

Zucker, J. (2020). Miscarriage happens to LGBTQ2 parents too. *Xtra Magazine,* https://xtra-magazine.com/health/miscarriage-lgbtq-parents-loss-177106

Raising Sunshine

ACKNOWLEDGEMENTS

I begin my thanks at the beginning with Mrs. Kathleen Ahern who had hope that the written words of a shy third grader would give the world a voice that was worth hearing and with Mr. John Griffin who helped to give that same teenage voice the courage to be heard.

I am forever grateful to all of those who have made it possible for me to write while raising a vivacious sunshine child and a spirited rainbow baby. For the Gustafsons who offered insight into the life of a writer and the process of writing. For Debbie who shouldered some domestic duties so that I could write. And for Greg and Aimee Wasinski, who let me crash at their idyllic Trilogy Retreat Center for a marathon editing weekend.

For those who, throughout my life, nurtured and grew my faith and for the people God unwittingly used to prepare me for Noemi's death, I am deeply grateful.

Of course, my family and I are forever in debt to the medical staff at Beth Israel Deaconess Medical Center who brought Noemi into the world and who did everything they could to keep us both alive – thank you for bearing the grief that I know you brought home with you that day and for your willingness to get up again the next day and keep caring for the patients that needed you.

I will never be able to fully express my gratitude for all of those who walked beside us during our grief and healing. Your prayers and love for us helped to heal us while simultaneously impressing on me how important community is. I am also forever grateful for all of those who visited us in the hospital and who helped with Noemi's burial Mass and funeral reception. There are too many of you to list here but be assured that not one of you went unnoticed and none are forgotten.

And of course, most of all, I am so incredibly grateful for the families God gave me at birth and through marriage:

- ✓ Irena and Zdenek - I am constantly thankful for the years of labor you put into raising your son and for your willingness to give him to me at great personal sacrifice.

✓ Pavel, Jan, Filip, Olga, Dana, Gabi, and all of my nieces and nephews – I am so appreciative of the ways that you cared for us as we grieved. Your prayers, thoughts, willingness to talk about my pain, artwork, time spent with us on vacations, and Facebook messages meant so much.

✓ Grammy and Grampy - your presence and support throughout my life has been a great blessing to me. You believe in me more than I believe in myself and I will always be grateful for your love, support and the memories we lived together and for the hours of stories supplied by your resident hobgoblin.

✓ Mimi and Papa - the faith that you passed onto your children and, thus, onto me, has been the only unshakable rock in my life and I look forward to Mimi crying tears of joy when we are united again and can share this amazing life story I am living.

✓ Alyssa - thank you for the ways you have supported me – for caring for my Sunshine during emergencies, for agreeing with me when I need someone to do so, and for offering me a fascinating glimpse into the world of art that is so foreign to our science/social science/mechanically minded family. You make our family stronger, gentler, and more fascinating.

✓ Dave - from the time we roamed the house arm in arm as detectives, you have been my constant friend. Your quiet, thoughtful presence has always been a sure support at the hardest times and your sarcastic humor has been a source of joy in the good ones. Thank you for being the person who made me want our daughter to have a sibling and thank you for the amazing uncle you are to the kiddos that call you Uncle Dump.

The deepest gratitude is often the most difficult to express. There are no words to adequately express my thanks to my parents, my Sunshine, and my Rainbow. Day-in and day-out, you have been my support and my cheerleaders – my dearest friends. But I would have to write another book to even begin to touch on the things I am grateful for about you. Perhaps someday I will, but for now, just know that I am thankful for all of it – from the endless breaded-chicken vacations to the deep love you have for our Father. My life is so much more precious because of each of you.

Jakub, there is no me without you. I am who I am because I am yours. You are the rock of our family who has held us together and turned us towards the Truth when everything was falling apart. You are, and always will be, my great love and my best friend. Because my thankfulness for you is endless but this book must end, I will have stop with this: thank you for taking my whipped cream and thereby changing my life. And looking back on it, I was right: I was falling in love with you and I'm glad you were in the same boat.

Finally, thanks to St. Azelie, a mother who knows my pain, penned words that gave me hope, and whose mothering of her sunshine and rainbow children yielded exceptional results. Please pray for me as I raise mine.

Raising Sunshine

APPENDIX I: DAILY SELF-CARE CHECKLIST

Morning	Take medicine	
	Have a big drink	
	Eat at least one healthy item	
	Wash-up, brush your hair, brush your teeth, change your clothes	
Noon	Have another big drink	
	Take medicine	
	Eat something that has protein and at least one fruit or vegetable	
Evening	Have yet another big drink	
	Take medicine	
	Eat something that has protein and at least one fruit or vegetable	
	Start your wind-down or bed-time routine	
	Get into bed at your usual time	
At Some Point During the Day	Get some exercise (even if all you can manage is a little walk around the house)	
	Do something you enjoy (even if it is something as little as savoring the smell of your shampoo)	
	Rest as often as you can	
	Tell yourself to put one foot in front of the other and keep going	

Raising Sunshine

APPENDIX II: MEDICATION CHART

Time	Medication	Dose	Time	Medication	Dose
12am			12pm		
1am			1pm		
2am			2pm		
3am			3pm		
4am			4pm		
5am			5pm		
6am			6pm		
7am			7pm		
8am			8pm		
9am			9pm		
10am			10pm		
11am			11pm		

Raising Sunshine

APPENDIX III: HORMONES – THE MAJOR PLAYERS

Progesterone	As its name suggests ("pro-ges*ation*") this is the hormone that gets the most credit for maintaining a pregnancy. After birth, progesterone levels plummet and the ovaries do not begin to produce more until the first postpartum menstruation. This disruption in levels may contribute to depression.
Estrogen	This sex hormone is responsible for many functions in the human body. After delivery, estrogen levels change dramatically to promote lactation. This can disrupt the amount of serotonin in the body which often leaves parents feeling emotionally and physically low.
Testosterone	While it is known for its role in male development, everyone has testosterone. Higher levels of testosterone seem to be linked to postpartum depression.
Thyroid Hormones	Thyroid hormones play a role in thinking abilities and are likely to impact our mood. Almost a quarter of postpartum parents have problems with their thyroids. As a result, many postpartum parents have emotional distress that is impacted by their thyroid hormones.
Stress Hormones (Like Cortisol)	Not surprisingly, an event like infant death triggers the production of stress hormones. Stress hormones are linked to a number of mental health issues including anxiety and depression. They are also known to contribute to physical health problems.
Serotonin	Known for its role in depression, low levels of serotonin can leave you feeling blue. The amount of serotonin your brain has available is influenced by several other hormones including estrogen.
Oxytocin	Informally, this hormone goes by the nickname "the feel-good hormone," and that is precisely what it is. Not only does it make us happy, oxytocin increases our ability to bond with one another. In the postpartum period, hormones are operating

	under the assumption that there is a baby that parents need to bond with. Unfortunately, our hormone levels do not automatically recalibrate after our babies die. As a result, oxytocin continues to be produced during lactation which is when most bonding would ordinarily occur. Fluctuations in oxytocin can cause moods to "yo-yo."
Dopamine	Dopamine plays a key role in our reward system. Simply put, it helps us to feel good when something good happens and it triggers us to want more. The way that our body produces and uses dopamine during the postpartum period changes in many ways. Additionally, dopamine is influenced by other hormones that are in flux at this time. These changes can leave parents susceptible to low moods and depression.

APPENDIX IV: BOOK LIST

BOOKS ABOUT INFANT LOSS

Always My Twin by Valerie Samuels

> This book is meant for children who lose a twin sibling. In addition to helping children to understand their loss, it includes space for journaling.

Ethan's Butterflies: A spiritual book for young children and parents after the loss of a baby by Christine Jonas-Simpson

> *Ethan's Butterflies* is the book that we found to be closest to my daughter's experience. Its child friendly pictures help to tell the story of a little elephant whose baby sibling died. It is a good conversation starter about things like burial, Heaven, and making sure that your infant remains part of your family. It is most appropriate for pre-school and young school-aged children.

Goodbye Sister: A Sibling's Book for Infant Loss by Kimberly Newton

> This book helps families to grieve together, accept their emotions, and acknowledge their grief in healthy ways.

My Sibling Still: For Those Who Have Lost a Sibling to Miscarriage, Stillbirth, and Infant Death by Megan Lacourrege

> Written for children who experience any kind of infant loss, this book helps children to embrace their role as a sibling - even after the baby has died. It helps families to find ways to remember their baby as part of their family.

Stacy Had a Little Sister by Wendie Old

> *Stacy Had a Little Sister* is the story of a little girl whose sister dies from SIDS. This book addresses the guilt that sunshine children often feel.

We Were Gonna Have a Baby, But We Had an Angel Instead by Pat Schwiebert

> Schwiebert uses concise language to let children know that their feelings and emotions are normal responses to the disappointment of not having a sibling. The book contains practical solutions for helping children through infant loss.

BOOKS ABOUT SIBLING LOSS IN GENERAL

Always My Brother by Jean Reagan

> This book helps children who feel guilty about enjoying life after their sibling has died. It also talks about how memories can keep loved ones in our lives after their death.

Bird by Zetta Elliot

> For older children, *Bird* tells the story of a boy who uses art to process his older brother's drug-related death.

Little Women by Louisa May Alcott

> There are several versions of this book so you can find one that is suitable for most ages. The story follows the growth of four sisters, one of whom dies when they are young adults. Due to the palpable love between the sisters, this death is deeply moving and touches on the unique relationship between sisters.

Where's Jess by Marvin Johnson

> *Where's Jess* helps children to understand the powerful emotions that they are feeling because of sibling loss. It is very straightforward, uses age-appropriate language and does not discuss religious aspects of death.

BOOKS ABOUT GRIEF IN GENERAL

A Christmas Carol by Charles Dickens

> Themes of grief and loss are woven throughout this classic tale (and many of Dickens' other tales). The scene that deals with Tiny Tim's death is probably the most potent, but much of Scrooge's decision to change rests on letting go of the bitterness he has built up because of past sorrows.

Annie and the Old One by Miska Miles

> This is the story of a Navajo girl who is struggling to understand that her grandmother will die. Her grandmother uses stories and legends to help her to comprehend death's inevitability.

Charlotte's Web by E.B. White

> This story uses animals to teach about loss and the cycle of life.

Harry Potter by J.K. Rowling

> All the books in the Harry Potter series deal with grief. In the early books, Harry wrestles with his feelings about his parents' death. In later books, beloved characters also die.

Someone I Love Died by Christine Tangvald

> This is an interactive book that offers children a Christian understanding of what happens to their loved ones after death.

Something Very Sad Happened: A Toddler's Guide to Understanding Death by Bonnie Zucker

This book is written in language that helps very young children to understand death. Its format allows parents to substitute words and names, personalizing the story.

Sprite Helps Say Goodbye by Kelly Oriard

Sprite Helps Say Goodbye is a board-book that helps children to learn about the many types of "goodbyes" we must say in life. It reassures them that their memories are ways to remain connected to those they love.

Tear Soup by Pat Schwiebert and Chuck DeKlyen

This book is about a grandmother who is dealing with the loss of her husband, shows how grief is a process that changes over time. It emphasizes that it is okay to be sad. At the end of the book are helpful grief "cooking tips" that offer useful information about grief. It is a beautifully illustrated book.

The Big Wave by Pearl Buck

The characters in this book wrestle with grief after a tsunami hits their Japanese town.

The Christmas Day Kitten by James Herriot

This sweet children's story tells the tale of a stray mother cat who finds a safe home for her kitten before her own death.

The Invisible String by Patrice Karsi

One of the more well-known children's books about grief, *The Invisible String* teaches children that even after death, they are connected to their loved one.

The Voyage of the Dawn Treader and *The Last Battle* by C.S. Lewis

Of all the books in the Chronicles of Narnia, my opinion is that *The Voyage of the Dawn Treader* and *The Last Battle* wrestle most clearly and directly with death and loss. Aslan's country offers the opportunity to think about life after death.

Water Bugs & Dragonflies by Doris Stickney and Gloria C. Ortiz

Water Bugs and Dragonflies is a fable that addresses the finality and unknowns of death in a hopeful way. It also helps to place death within the context of natural life. It is appropriate for all ages, though younger children may not understand the metaphor between the bugs and death.

When Someone Very Special Dies Children Can Learn to Cope with Grief by Marge Heegaard

This is a combination of a storybook and workbook that helps children understand the life cycle and their own responses to grief. It builds their ability to express their emotions while also teaching other coping skills.

Where the Red Fern Grows by Wilson Rawls

This is a classic book that uses animals to teach important lessons about life and death. There is a sibling death in the book, but the primary source of grief is the death of a beloved dog.

APPENDIX V: FAMOUS PEOPLE WHO LOST SIBLINGS

Carl Anderson

Carl Anderson, an actor, and musician who is best known for his role as Judas Iscariot in the Broadway Musical *Jesus Christ, Superstar*, had a twin brother who passed away at the age of 11 months due to a bronchial infection.

Dietrich Bonhoeffer

Theologian and vocal opponent to the Nazis, Dietrich Bonhoeffer lost his older brother to fighting in World War I. Bonhoeffer was a child at the time. According to some accounts, the Bonhoeffer family gave the brother's bible to Dietrich Bonhoeffer and the future theologian used this Bible throughout his life.

George W. Bush

George W. Bush, the 43rd President of the United States, lost his little sister to leukemia when she was three years old. His sister was such a well-known part of their family that when George Bush Sr. died, cartoonist Marshall Ramsey drew a picture of her with both of her parents in Heaven.

Stephen Colbert

Known for his comedy and humor, Stephen Colbert was ten years old when his father and two older siblings died in the crash of Eastern Airlines Flight 212. As an adult, he said his mother influenced his own ability to grieve: "By her example, I am not bitter. By *her* example, she was not. Broken, yes. Bitter, no. It was a very healthy reciprocal acceptance of suffering. Which does not mean defeated by suffering. Acceptance is not defeat. Acceptance is just awareness."

Marie Curie

The first woman to win a Nobel Prize, Marie Curie's older sister died from typhus while Marie Curie was a school-aged child. Her research on radiation changed the world in many ways. Albert Einstein, perhaps reflecting on her generosity, once said "Marie Curie is, of all celebrated beings, the only one whom fame has not corrupted."

Charles Dickens

Charles Dickens had a difficult childhood in many ways. As a boy, his family was held in debtors' prison and he worked in a factory to provide for them. Dickens also experienced the death of two younger siblings during his early life. His writings - which drove societal changes that helped the poor - often reflect the themes of struggle and loss that he himself experienced.

Sigmund Freud

Given my background in psychology, I could not leave out Sigmund Freud. Freud is one of the most influential figures in modern psychology. When his younger brother, Julius, died at 18 months old, it had a big impact on Freud. As an adult, Freud recalled feeling envious and angry at his brother and many psychologists believe that these feelings likely contributed to Freud's work on sibling rivalry and guilt.

Ruth Bader Ginsburg

The first Jewish woman and second woman ever to serve as a justice of the United States Supreme Court, Ruth Bader Ginsburg lost her older sister when she was a little over a year old. Her legendary career led to significant advancements in gender equality.

Johann Wolfgang von Goethe

Johann Wolfgang von Goethe was a famous German writer who is best known for writing *Faust*. Five of his younger siblings died as children.

Jackie, Tito, Jermaine, and Marlon Jackson

The four oldest Jackson siblings (whose musical talent gave them the moniker, the "First Family of Soul,") lost an infant sibling, Brandon. The baby was Marlon Jackson's twin and was born the year before Michael Jackson's birth.

Caroline Kennedy

The daughter of President Kennedy, Caroline Kennedy is an author and attorney who was the Ambassador to Japan for four years. She was born after the death of her stillborn sister, Arabella. When she was six years old, her brother Patrick died when he was just two days old. His very public birth and death led to an increase in lifesaving medical treatment for premature infants.

Coretta Scott King

The wife of Dr. Martin Luther King, Jr., Coretta Scott King was also a singer, speaker, and civil rights activist in her own right. Her older sister, Eunice, died as a child, though little information about her is available.

John Kinsel, Sr.

John Kinsel, Sr. is best known for his work as a Navajo Code Talker. He used his knowledge of the English and Navajo languages to send secret messages during

World War II, giving the United States an advantage in the Pacific theater. His younger brother died.

Abraham Lincoln

As depicted in the introduction to this book, President Lincoln lost an infant sibling at birth during his childhood. The memory stayed with him throughout his life and he eventually mentioned it in his autobiography.

Martin Luther

In many ways, Martin Luther was the man who was responsible for the Protestant Reformation. Like many people who lived in the late 1400s, Martin Luther lost several siblings during his childhood.

Pope St. John Paul II

Known as one of the greatest religious leaders of our time, Pope St. John Paul II was the youngest of three children. His older sister died before his birth. When Pope St. John Paul II was a school-aged child, his brother died while caring for patients with scarlet fever. The loss of his brother was particularly difficult for Pope St. John Paul II. He once said: "After her (my mother's) death and, later, the death of my older brother, I was left alone with my father, a deeply religious man. Day after day I was able to observe the austere way in which he lived...his example was in a way my first seminary, a kind of domestic seminary."

Elvis Presley

Legendary singer Elvis Presley had an identical twin brother who was stillborn. Not surprisingly, Elvis was extremely close to his mother in part because of this loss. Unfortunately, according to many accounts, their relationship was overly close to the point that it was unhealthy.

Diego Rivera

Known as one of Mexico's most influential painters, Diego Rivera's twin brother died when they were around two years old. A year later, Rivera began drawing. His art became famous for reflecting Mexican history, the cultural changes that surrounded him, and his political beliefs (which were controversial). He painted murals because he believed that everyone should be able to access and enjoy art.

Eleanor Roosevelt

America's longest serving first lady and an icon of human rights, Eleanor Roosevelt lost her mother and younger brother at the age of eight. She was orphaned at the age of ten. Despite these early losses, or perhaps because of them, she became a compassionate champion of the suffering.

Elizabeth Ann Seton

The first American to be recognized as a saint, Elizabeth Ann Seton founded the first religious order of Catholic women in America and the first Catholic schools in the United States. Consequently, she became the patron saint of Catholic schools. Elizabeth Seton's mother died giving birth to her little sister. When Elizabeth was four years old, this sister also died.

Ed Sullivan

Ed Sullivan was an American entertainer known for "The Ed Sullivan Show" which was a variety show that featured exceptionally talented artists. The show ran for almost twenty years. Ed Sullivan had a twin brother, Daniel, who was not healthy and died when he was a few months old.

Amy Tan

A well-known American writer, Amy Tan's brother and father died from brain tumors when she was fifteen years old. As a teenager, Tan learned that her mother had been previously married and that she had five siblings from that marriage (two of whom died before Tan was born). This realization was part of Tan's inspiration for her book *The Joy Luck Club*.

Kateri Tekakwitha

St. Kateri, the first Native American to be canonized as a Saint, lost her immediate family (including her infant brother) during an outbreak of smallpox. She was four years old at the time of her family's death and was raised by her uncle.

Betsie ten Boom

Betsie ten Boom was the daughter of famed watchmaker Casper ten Boom who, along with Betsie and her sister Corrie, was arrested for helping Jews escape from the Nazi occupied Netherlands. Betsie died in a concentration camp. Her sister, Corrie, survived and became a writer and speaker. Years before the family's heroic act, Betsie's baby brother, Hendrik Jan, died when he was just a few months old.

Therese of Lisieux's Three Oldest Sisters

St. Therese of Lisieux was the youngest child in a family that lost four children during infancy. Her three oldest sisters were all still children when they lost their siblings. Each of them grew up to join religious orders and one of them, Leonie, was beatified. Their mother, St. Zelie Martin was deeply impacted by the death of her babies and her letters include beautiful passages about them.

Mark Twain

Mark Twain was the penname for Samuel Langhorne Clemens, an American author who is best known for his book *The Adventures of Tom Sawyer*. Clemens older brother died in infancy. Another older brother and an older sister died during his childhood.

APPENDIX VI: ART THAT EXPLORES DEATH

Music

- *Classical Music for the Requiem Mass*
  Requiems were written for Catholic Masses for the dead. Many of the great composers wrote them, including Mozart, Verdi, Berlioz, Bruckner, and Dvorak. While they were traditionally intended for religious settings, today they are enjoyed by people of all faiths.

- *Home – Grief Songs for Kids*
  Featuring various artists, this album contains religious songs that are focused on grief and is intended for children.

- *Hymns*
  These are the songs that have filled the Church for generations. Some, like "Amazing Grace," are well-known even outside of Christian circles. Others, like "How Great Thou Art," are traditional funeral songs within the Church. Yet, there are many other beautiful hymns about death that are less well known and worth exploring. While the music and words of the hymns are moving on their own, finding out the story of how they were written is often equally powerful. "It Is Well with My Soul," for instance, was written by Horatio Spafford after his four daughters died in a shipwreck, making these words of the hymn even more powerful: *"When sorrows like sea billows roll, whatever my lot, Thou hast taught me to say, 'It is well, it is well with my soul.'"*

- *Manawa Wera haka*
  The Maori people of New Zealand use traditional dances and chants, called haka, to mark important events. The Manawa Wera haka is often used at funerals.

- *Modern Christian Worship Songs*
  Many modern worship music composers have faced grief and they include this in their songs. Steven Curtis Chapman lost his young daughter and wrote several songs about his grief, including *Heaven is the Face*. The list of worship songs

would be far too long to include here, but a quick Google search will provide you with a list of songs to listen to with your sunshine child.

- *New Orleans Jazz Funerals*
  These are marches that occur during funerals in New Orleans. Mourning music begins solemnly and then becomes increasingly lively. Like much of New Orleans' culture, jazz funerals combine West African, Haitian, and colonial traditions.

- *Loch Lomond*
  This is a haunting Scottish song that deals with death and the hope of reunification in times of war.

Fine Art

- After the Storm (Sarah Bernhardt)

- Ancient Egyptian Statues (Egypt)

- Angel of Grief (William Story)

- Death in the Sickroom (Edvard Munch)

- Inconsolable Grief (Ivan Kramskoy)

- Kutna Hora Bone Chapel (Czech Republic)

- La Dia de los Muertos heads (Day of the Dead)

- Melancolie (Albert Gyorgy)

- Memento Mori (assorted art meant to remind viewers of their own mortality)

- Precious in His Sight (Greg Olsen)

- Sorrowing Old Man (Van Gogh)

- Stations of the Cross (various representations)

- Taj Mahal (India)

- The Pieta (Michelangelo)

Theater and Television

- *A Christmas Carol* (multiple versions)
- *Bambi* (1942)
- *Bluey: "Copycat"* (2018)
- *Big Hero 6* (2014)
- *Charlotte's Web* (2006)
- *Chronicles of Narnia* (2005-2010)
- *Creature Fixers: Country Vets (2020 – present)*
- *Sesame Street: "Farewell, Mr. Hooper* (1983)
- *Soul* (2020)
- *Encanto* (2021)
- *Frozen* (2013)
- *Harry Potter* (2001-2010)
- *Hachi: A Dog's Tale* (2009)
- *Hocus Pocus 2* (2022)
- *Les Miserables* (2012)
- *Little Women* (1994 or 2019)
- *Mr. Roger's Neighborhood: "Death of a Goldfish" (1970)*
- *Nature Documentaries* (assorted)
- *Old Yeller* (1957)
- *Pokemon Origins: "File 2: Cubone"* (2013)
- *Soul* (2020)
- *Star Wars* (assorted release dates)

- *The Grave of the Fireflies* (1988) (Only appropriate for older teens)

- *The Lion King* (1994 or 2019)

- *The Secret Garden* (1993)

- *The Secret of NIMH* (1982)

- *The Snow Man* (1982)

- *Where the Red Fern Grows* (1974)

APPENDIX VII: TROUBLESOME THOUGHT CHALLENGE FOR ANGER AND ANXIETY

What do you do when your brain goofs and tells you to be afraid or angry for no good reason? You follow the steps below to fix your troublesome thought (TBT):

Zero In

Figure out what thought you have that is causing you to feel anxious. Sometimes, just the act of identifying your TBT can help you to feel better.

Fight Back

Think logically about your TBT. Argue against it. Tell yourself why your TBT is irrational or incorrect. You must be honest with yourself – don't be overly optimistic or dismiss real concerns. Just think rationally about your TBT without being swayed by the emotions it causes you.

Count the Costs

You might think that thoughts and beliefs are cheap, but the reality is that they can come at a high cost. They can rob you of your peace of mind, deprive you and those around you of relationships, and limit your experiences and opportunities. The chances are good that your TBT is not worth its cost and recognizing this can make it easier to let go of it when you...

Replace It

Replace the TBT with a thought that is more realistic. You get bonus points if it is also realistically optimistic (for example: "she might fall off of the bike but if she does, she won't die, and she might even learn something"). You might want to use the arguments you made in step two as you develop a good replacement thought.

What is the thought/belief that is setting off your anxiety alarms?	Why is this TBT wrong or irrational?	What does this TBT cost?	What is a more realistic thought/belief?
- My child's illness might be much more than a common cold - I wouldn't know since I didn't even realize how sick my baby was	-There are many children in her class who are sick -Kids get sick ALL THE TIME -My daughter is ok right now -My judgment about this is not powerful enough to cause her death	-My daughter might pick up on my anxiety and become anxious -Anxiety will make it harder for her to fight the virus -I might be teaching my child to worry about things she should not be worried about -I won't be able to be well-rested and care for my child if I keep worrying	This is most likely just a typical childhood illness and she will get better without any trouble. Even if she doesn't, I know what to look for in case she needs help and she has a good medical team who will care for her well

What is the thought/belief that is setting off your anxiety alarms?	Why is this TBT wrong or irrational?	What does this TBT cost?	What is a more realistic thought/belief?

Raising Sunshine

APPENDIX VIII: RELAXATION EXERCISES

5,4,3,2,1	This exercise is good for breaking the cycle of anxiety by focusing on the present. You start by identifying five things that you see, five things that you feel, and five things that you hear. Then you do the same thing again but this time you only identify four things for each sensation. Now do it again and list three things, then two and then one. Do not worry if you cannot list enough sensations, just focus on the things you are perceiving in the moment.
Breathing Exercises	Did you know that the way you breathe can make an enormous difference in how you feel? In fact, if you want to relax, focusing on your breaths is one of your best options. Anxiety relieving breaths fill up your belly (your stomach moves out while your shoulders stay still) and should be slow and deep. One of my favorite breath exercises for kids is to have them take a deep breath to smell an imaginary warm cookie and then they blow out to cool down a pretend mug of hot chocolate. Another favorite is to imagine lying on a hammock and breathing in while the hammock swings one way and then breathing out as the hammock swings in the other direction. You can use whatever imagery works best for you.
Square Breathing	This is like the last exercise except that it does not require as much imagination. Instead, you tell yourself that each breath draws one of the four sides in a square. In other words, you: ✓ Inhale for four seconds as your breath makes the top line. ✓ Exhale for four seconds while your breath makes a side. ✓ Inhale for another four seconds as your breath draws the bottom.

	✓ Exhale for four seconds while your breath makes the final side. You can keep making "squares" like this until your breathing is calm and slow.
Warm Sunshine	This is my personal favorite. For this exercise, you sit comfortably and close your eyes. Then imagine yourself at a beach with the warm sun rays beating down on you. The beams are warming and loosening your muscles as you envision them moving progressively down your body from the top of your head to the tip of your toes. You can imagine the rays lingering in places where you are holding stress (often the neck, shoulders, jaw, or hands) and creating extra warmth and looseness in those areas.
Progressive Tense and Release	Like Warm Sunshine, this exercise starts at the top of your head and works all the way down to your toes. You start by tensing the muscles of your scalp as tightly as you can, holding for a count of five and then releasing. Then you repeat the process for the muscles of your face, then your neck, and so on down your body. By the time you finish, you should have tensed and released all of your muscles.
Rapid Tense and Release	If you do not have time to do the Progressive Tense and Release exercise, you can take a shortcut. Tense all of your muscles at once. Squeeze them as tightly as you can (don't forget your face and toes) and hold for five seconds. Then relax your whole body simultaneously and enjoy feeling a little like jelly.
Safe Place	If you have the time and want to use your imagination, going to your "safe place" is a fun relaxation exercise to use. Start by making sure you are in a comfortable position with as few distractions as possible. Close your eyes. Next, think about your favorite safe and calm place. Imagine that you are there all by yourself with no demands or expectations. It is just you in this place. Imagine all the details of your surroundings.

	What does it smell like? What things can you hear? What things can you see? Is it warm? What are you feeling? Once you are done relaxing in your happy place, start to wiggle your body and bring your focus back to the sensations that your body is feeling. Then slowly open your eyes and let yourself come back to our world.
Mantras	Some people find it helpful to silently repeat a certain phrase or prayer whenever they find themselves feeling anxious. These range from, "I'm OK," or "I've got this," to repeating a religious word or a line from a song that brings comfort. As someone who has struggled with obsessive compulsive disorder in the past, I tend not to use this technique because it too easily becomes a compulsion for me, but many people (my daughter included) find it helpful.

Raising Sunshine

ENDNOTES

PREFACE

[1] This is a fictional account based on real events that happened in Abraham Lincoln's life. The 16th president of the United States really did lose an infant sibling and recorded this loss in his autobiography.

[2] When an infant dies, there are many adults who help the surviving sibling to navigate their loss including birth parents, stepparents, grandparents, aunts, uncles, cousins and family friends. For the sake of simplicity, this book will use the term parent when talking about these caregivers since parents (including step and foster parents) are often the most immediate support people in children's lives.

[3] Fletcher, et al. 2012

[4] Van & Meleis, 2003

CHAPTER TWO

[5] For several years after my daughter's death, I edited my daughter's books to make them match my family's situation. Books that talked about the death of other family members or friends upset my Sunshine because they reminded her that other people she loved could die, too. Other books talked about religious and spiritual beliefs that we do not share. I found that many of these stories could be easily altered so that they fit our needs.

[6] Appendix IV of this book contains a list of books that deal with death and grief. The list is not exhaustive, but I hope that it helps you to get started on your search.

[7] To jumpstart your journey of grief through art, Appendix VI contains a list of art that has helped my own friends and family on their journeys through grief.

CHAPTER THREE

[8] Our language does not have a word that adequately names the time when a Sunshine child first sees their deceased sibling. I use the words "meet" and "introduction" in this section, though neither word is truly appropriate for this event.

[9] This belief was somewhat contradictory since it was also generally assumed that children do not grieve.

[10] Older children often have insight into their own grief needs and, whenever possible, these should be respected. Many professionals feel that, after the age of about three or four years, children can usually make their own decisions about their participation in grief rituals. Some people who work with grieving children even feel that many children can make these decisions by the age of two. Parents frequently find that this is sound advice. For example, bereaved parents Susan Scrimshaw and Daniel March

"...found that allowing (their Sunshine) to take the lead in what she needed to do with (the baby) was more valuable than (they) ever could have predicted."

CHAPTER FOUR
[11] Organizations like *Now I Lay Me Down to Sleep* (nowilaymedowntosleep.org) offer free professional photography services to families whose babies have died or are dying. Some hospitals also have staff that are trained to provide sensitive, professional photography in these situations.

[12] There are many programs that provide blankets and clothing to dying and deceased infants. *Sunshine State Angel Gowns* (myangelgowns.com) is one such organization. Your hospital may also have a collection of donated baby items that you can use to clothe and swaddle your baby.

CHAPTER SIX
[13] There are, of course, several reasons that I do not recommend this approach to dealing with the baby's possessions. Apart from the safety issues involved, Prince's decision to burn his son's possessions meant that his wife was left without the physical reminders of the baby she wanted. This situation emphasizes the importance of considering the ways in which our grief-motivated decisions can impact those around us.

[14] Funk, et al. 2018

[15] Apart from the things that my Sunshine wanted to keep, we held onto a few of Noemi's things that were most special to us as her parents. For example, her crib quilt now hangs as a wall decoration.

CHAPTER SEVEN
[16] When Noemi died, I called our sunshine daughter's extra-curricular teachers to tell them what had happened. None of them ever said anything to my Sunshine unless she herself mentioned her sister's death. However, each of them made a point of subtly reaching out to her in their own way. Some sat next to her more frequently during circle time, others made a point of seeking her out for high-fives during sports classes, and a few patted her head or shoulder, reassuringly. As a result of these interactions, my daughter's relationships with her teachers grew at a time when she needed their extra support.

SECTION II
[17] I want to be clear that it is more challenging for some of us to overcome our loss than it is for others. I have heard it said that we are all in the same storm, but not the same boat. Some of us have more physical and emotional resources to help us deal with our loss. Others face additional hardships that complicate our grief and make it harder to overcome our sorrow. However, each of us can choose whether we allow the pain and bitterness of our loss to prevent us from taking the next step towards healing and embracing the life we have.

CHAPTER EIGHT

[18] If the experts' advice does not reassure you, let me offer you some solidarity: if you come by my house, you will see kids running around in bare feet, covered in mud, and eating pancakes for dinner. They will be working on some project in the yard like digging a river where their dad has been trying to grow the lawn or making time machines in the woods. They have never had a bento box lunch and are used to opening their lunchbox to find a few cheese sticks and some whole wheat bread. Sometimes, we forget to empty what remains of those lunches and discover how quickly ants can find our mistakes. However, the laundry piles are (mostly) clean, my kids live passionately, and they have awesome immune systems!

[19] Najman and his colleagues offer a good overview of research related to marriages and infant death in their 1993 article, "The Impact of Child Death on Marital Adjustment."

CHAPTER NINE
[20] Sadly, there are times when parents' relationships are harmful and potentially dangerous to all involved. If you are feeling threatened or unsafe in your relationship, it is important that you take steps to protect yourself and your child right away. See end note 23 for resources.

[21] These "dates" involved doing something besides renting a movie and eating take-out at home, though that can be time well-spent, too, and we certainly do that a lot in my own home.

[22] This advice relies on the assumption that your relationship is not abusive. If your partner abuses or mistreats you, changing your behavior will not stop the abuse. You do not deserve to be mistreated in your relationships. For information about getting help, see endnote 23.

[23] If you do not feel safe in your relationship, help for you and your sunshine child is available. If either of you is in immediate physical danger, call 911. If you need help, but danger is not imminent, the National Domestic Violence Hotline can be reached at 800-799-SAFE (7233) or by texting "START" to 88788. The advocates who respond to your call are trained to help you to think through your situation and brainstorm ways to ensure that you and your sunshine child are safe. Before calling, make sure that you are in a safe place, away from your abuser. After calling, delete the conversations and phone numbers from your phone so that your abuser does not find them.

CHAPTER TEN
[24] Sandra Blakeslee and V.S. Ramachandran wrote a fascinating book about this phenomenon called *Phantoms in the Brain*. If you're a science geek like me, it is a great read!

[25] In fact, in some cases pregnancy can occur before periods return.

[26] While these suggestions can be helpful, the truth is that time will be your greatest asset. You may always find yourself looking at little children and wondering about who your child could have been, but the searing pain that you are currently experiencing will eventually lessen. Now, six years after Noemi's death, I can sit

behind a little dark-haired first grader at my Sunshine's school and imagine for a moment that she is my Noemi. But such "what if" moments are less painful.

[27] It goes without saying that there are some relationships that are truly toxic and in which someone may try to use their friend's grief to feel better about themselves or to injure their friend more deeply. If the person who has hurt you has a pattern of being spiteful towards you or those around them, you should establish appropriate boundaries to protect yourself from this person, particularly at this time when you are vulnerable.

CHAPTER ELEVEN
[28] These risks include seizures, blood clots, paralysis and even death.

[29] It usually takes between two and three weeks for most of your milk supply to dry up, but milk may continue leaking for some time after that.

[30] A less common donation option is donating your milk to research. You can run a quick internet search to find research organizations that are accepting breast milk donations. At the time of writing, one such organization was Mommy's Milk Human Milk Research Biorepository (https://mommysmilkresearch.org).

[31] Draining your breasts completely tells your body to produce more milk.

[32] You can do this in one of three ways: eliminate one pumping session per day, pump less frequently, or decrease the amount of time you spend pumping.

[33] Check with your hospital team to see if your insurance will cover the cost of a pump.

[34] Avoid underwire to prevent mastitis.

[35] If you do not have a pump, you can hand express your milk by massaging from the outer edges in toward your nipples. You may want to use cream or warm water to lubricate your skin and help to get the milk flowing.

[36] You will know that a plugged duct has released when a stream of milk begins to squirt from an area that was previously not producing milk and you begin to feel a release of pressure. Even after a duct has released, it may remain sore while inflammation subsides.

[37] Mastitis often responds quickly to antibiotics but, left untreated, it can result in a breast abscess. Thus, it is essential that you get medical care as quickly as possible.

[38] This may mean that you must hold off on plans to suppress your milk supply. That is okay.

CHAPTER THIRTEEN
[39] The following websites can help you to find mental health care providers and supportive communities that are sensitive to the needs of patients from minority groups: Therapyforblackgirls.com, Sistersinloss.com, rtzhope.org/bipoc, https://www.asianmhc.org/therapists-us/, https://latinxtherapy.com/, and https://www.psychologytoday.com/us/therapists/native-american.

---

[40] When we miscarried a baby after Noemi, the hospital did not want to release the remains to us for burial. The funeral home that had helped us with Noemi ended up being instrumental in getting this second baby's remains from the hospital so that we could bury her beside her sister.

[41] In full disclosure, my husband is an employee of Cleveland Clinic, which is how I know about this program. However, neither he or I have any personal connection to or experience with this program.

[42] Unfortunately, in some families, one of the co-parents is unwilling or unable to parent in a healthy or appropriate way. This may mean that for the sake of your sunshine child, your goal needs to be protecting yourself rather than figuring out how to work together as a co-parenting team. If this is the case, you may benefit from working with a family therapist who can help you to figure out how to set important boundaries that will work for your family.

[43] This is particularly true for parents who lost both their baby and their partner due to complications with pregnancy or childbirth.

[44] Just in case you are tempted to do so, now is not the time to worry about being a burden – you need others to walk with you as you carry the burden of grief.

[45] This advice only applies to offers of help from people who are emotionally and physically safe for you and your child. If there are any safety concerns about the individual offering help, listen to you intuition and do not put yourself or your Sunshine at risk.

[46] When I was just a day old, my mother was asked to complete a survey about me. She described me as intense, which she correctly picked up on from my in-utero behaviors. During her next pregnancy, she was similarly accurate in her suspicion that my brother was much more laidback.

CHAPTER FIFTEEN

[47] This is also a good reminder to keep dangerous tools away from little hands!

[48] While it is normal and understandable to experience anger after a baby dies, it is never okay to express that anger in a violent way. If you are concerned about your ability to keep those around you safe due to your anger, or if you are afraid that you yourself might be unsafe because of a loved one's anger, please seek help immediately.

[49] Unfortunately, to make an animal feel helpless, they need to be subjected to something unpleasant. In this case, the mice were unable to escape from shocks that were administered to their tails.

[50] Hammack, et al. 2012

[51] Volpicelli, et al. 1995

---

[52] APA, 2017

[53] SoulCore is a combination of prayer and movements that stretch and strengthen the body.

[54] In most cases, siblings play no role at all in an infant's death, but I include them here because rarely they do. In these situations, thinking about their limits can be helpful for them. Of course, the reality is that, regardless of actual guilt, most sunshine children do feel guilty about their sibling's death. Often this is because of misunderstandings or magical thinking (for example, they may believe that their angry wish that there was no baby caused the baby to die). Children often hold onto these feelings of guilt as tenaciously as we do, so it is important to address them thoughtfully and not just dismiss them as unreasonable or irrational.

CHAPTER SIXTEEN
[55] Thinking about dying and wishing to die is very common after a loss. While it can be reassuring to know that such thoughts are not unusual, it is important to take them seriously. If you are concerned that you or someone you love may act on these thoughts, please get help right away. In the United States, you can call the National Suicide Prevention Line at 988 or, if you are concerned that suicide is imminent, contact emergency services at 911 and do not leave the person you are concerned about alone. If you are not concerned about an immediate risk of suicide, but you or a loved one is experiencing troubling thoughts, you can contact your primary care doctor, pediatrician, or mental health provider for guidance on how to get help.

[56] Rosen, 1987

[57] As your child works through their grief, you may need to balance their need for you with your own need to protect your emotions. Watching or hearing a child actively process their loss can be agonizing. For me, as difficult as it was, I felt that the importance of my daughter being able to work through her grief trumped my own desire to avoid her games. I learned to seek support from friends so that I could tolerate her play. Fortunately, I was lucky that my daughter did some of this processing with my mother, which gave me a break. In hindsight, I am glad that I let her process her grief in the way that she did because it allowed both of us to share the burden of her loss together.

[58] Picoult, *My Sister's Keeper*, 2004

[59] Separation anxiety is not unusually in children, even when they are not wrestling with the trauma of sibling death. It is not surprising, therefore, that grieving children have more difficulty separating from their parents.

[60] Regression is when a child who used to be able to do something no longer does it. For example, a child who was toilet trained may start having accidents or a child who was sleeping through the night may begin waking up crying.

[61] Children who are unhappy for any reason tend to express their distress by acting in ways that get them into trouble. It is not unusual for grieving children to be defiant,

aggressive, or otherwise difficult to manage. The good news is that such behaviors should be transient and lessen as the Sunshine processes their grief.

[62] Phobias are unrealistic or extreme fears of specific things. Grieving children may fear things related to sibling death, but they also may develop seemingly unrelated phobias.

[63] One of the most frightening things a parent can face is a suicidal child. The next chapter addresses signs that your child may need emergency care. Because it cannot be repeated often enough, if you think your child may be suicidal, call 988 or 911 and do not leave them alone until help arrives.

CHAPTER SEVENTEEN
[64] The criteria in this table were taken from the American Psychiatric Association's Diagnostic manual (the *DSM-5*). This manual contains the guidelines that clinicians use to diagnose their patients.

[65] American Addiction Centers, 2022

[66] If you are concerned that your child has overdosed, call 911 immediately. If you are concerned that they consumed something that could be poisonous, call poison control at 1-800-222-1222.

[67] While we usually think of people attempting suicide via overdoses, self-injury or hangings, young children who attempt suicide may do so in uncommon ways. For example, some young children who are suicidal deliberately run in front of moving vehicles or jump from high places. If your child does something dangerous, ask them why they did it. Their answer will help you to tease out whether they were just being impulsive and using poor judgment or if they were feeling suicidal.

[68] Due to the possibility that emergency responders may not be prepared to handle a mental health crisis appropriately, calling the new 988 number is preferable. This number will connect you to trained counselors who work to stabilize the person in crisis in the least disruptive way possible. For most of these calls, contacting 988 will allow you to avoid interacting with potentially unprepared law enforcement officers all together. In fact, less than 2% of the calls made to the hotline result in dispatching emergency services.

CHAPTER EIGHTEEN
[69] For simplicity's sake, I have chosen to use the term "God" from this point on.

[71] In almost all of the studies discussed in this chapter, the term religion is used to refer to any spiritual framework, including atheism. All such beliefs provide their adherents with a worldview through which they can make sense of their life experiences and, for the sake of this discussion, their loss. If a particular study focused on a specific form of religious belief, then I have identified that.

[72] Bakker, et al. 2013

[73] Goldstein, 2018

[74] Bakker, et al. 2013

[75] Bakker, et al. 2013

[76] It was not clear to researchers why this effect was found in Catholic children specifically.

[77] Cowhock, et al. 2011

[78] Kersting, et al. 2007

[79] Man, et al. 2008

[80] Van, et al. 2003

[81] Van, et al. 2003

[82] Van, et al. 2003

[83] Bakker, et al. 2013

[84] Bakker, et al. 2013

[85] Bakker, et al. 2013

[86] Bakker, et al. 2013

[87] Balk, 1983

[88] Bakker, et al. 2013

[89] Herberman, et al. 2013

[90] Bakker, et al. 2013

[91] Bakker, et al. 2013

[92] Often, the comfort that religions provide is connected to promises for the future. For example, when Noemi died, our neighbors were a devout Muslim family. The father once told me that he believes that when a child dies, God sees the mother's suffering and rewards her with Paradise.

[93] Harvard, 2018

[94] This is quite possibly the worst piece of advice for a school psychologist to ever give, but I have found that what sounded good in my textbooks does not always pan out when my children are in public places, especially when a level of quiet attention is expected!

[95] Harvard, 2018

[96] If you are interested in learning more about the ways that my faith has impacted my family and our journey through grief, I invite you to visit my blog at *mysustaininggrace.com*.

[97] McNess, 2007

[98] McNess, 2007

[99] Rosen, 1987

[100] Rosen, 1987

[101] McNess, 2007

CHAPTER NINETEEN
[102] For a more extensive list of famous people who lost siblings, see Appendix V.

Made in the USA
Las Vegas, NV
29 March 2025

20281374R00149